ROUTLEDGE LIBRARY EDITIONS:
JOURNALISM

Volume 4

THE UNITED STATES NEWSPAPER PROGRAM

THE UNITED STATES NEWSPAPER PROGRAM
Cataloging Aspects

Edited by
RUTH C. CARTER

LONDON AND NEW YORK

First published in 1986

This edition first published in 2016
by Routledge
2 Park Square, Milton Park, Abingdon, Oxon OX14 4RN

and by Routledge
711 Third Avenue, New York, NY 10017

Routledge is an imprint of the Taylor & Francis Group, an informa business

© 1986 The Haworth Press, Inc.

All rights reserved. No part of this book may be reprinted or reproduced or utilised in any form or by any electronic, mechanical, or other means, now known or hereafter invented, including photocopying and recording, or in any information storage or retrieval system, without permission in writing from the publishers.

Trademark notice: Product or corporate names may be trademarks or registered trademarks, and are used only for identification and explanation without intent to infringe.

British Library Cataloguing in Publication Data
A catalogue record for this book is available from the British Library

ISBN: 978-1-138-80197-4 (Set)
ISBN: 978-1-315-68235-8 (Set) (ebk)
ISBN: 978-1-138-92841-1 (Volume 4) (hbk)
ISBN: 978-1-138-92842-8 (Volume 4) (pbk)
ISBN: 978-1-315-68174-0 (Volume 4) (ebk)

Publisher's Note
The publisher has gone to great lengths to ensure the quality of this reprint but points out that some imperfections in the original copies may be apparent.

Disclaimer
The publisher has made every effort to trace copyright holders and would welcome correspondence from those they have been unable to trace.

The United States Newspaper Program: Cataloging Aspects

Ruth C. Carter
Editor

The Haworth Press
New York • London

The United States Newspaper Program: Cataloging Aspects has also been published as *Cataloging & Classification Quarterly,* Volume 6, Number 4, Summer 1986.

© 1986 by The Haworth Press, Inc. All rights reserved. No part of this book may be reproduced or utilized in any form or by any means, electronic or mechanical, including photocopying, microfilm and recording, or by any information storage and retrieval system, without permission in writing from the publisher. Printed in the United States of America.

The Haworth Press, Inc., 28 East 22 Street, New York, NY 10010-6194
EUROSPAN/Haworth, 3 Henrietta Street, London WC2E 8LU England

Library of Congress Cataloging in Publication Data

The United States newspaper program.

   (Cataloging & classification quarterly ; v. 6, no. 4)
   Bibliography: p.
   1. Cataloging of newspapers. 2. Newspaper and periodical libraries—United States.
3. American newspapers—Bibliography—Methodology. I. Carter, Ruth C. II. Series.
Z693.A15C35   vol. 6, no. 4   025.3 s   86-4828
[Z695.655]   [025.3'432]
ISBN 0-86656-576-0

The United States Newspaper Program: Cataloging Aspects

Cataloging & Classification Quarterly
Volume 6, Number 4

CONTENTS

Foreword	1
Jeffrey Field	
EDITORIAL	5
The National Endowment for the Humanities and the United States Newspaper Program	7
Harold Cannon	
Coordination of Cataloging Practices in the United States Newspaper Program	15
Robert B. Harriman, Jr.	
Status of Bibliographic Control	16
Suitable Clothing Required	19
How Ya Gonna Keep 'Em Down in Tech Services . . .	19
Getting Organized	21
Making It Work	23
Following Through	27
Challenges of On-Site Cataloging	31
Rebecca A. Wilson	
Lydia Suzanne Kellerman	
Introduction	31
Background	32
Pre-Site Visit Preparations	32
Initial On-Site Activities	33
Cataloging, Related Problems and Possible Solutions	33
Working Conditions	37
Conclusions	37

Perspectives on the Pennsylvania Newspaper Project at the University of Pittsburgh   39
Faye Leibowitz
Cathy Sorensen

Introduction	39
Cataloging Sites	40
Training	41
Identifying Procedures	42
Locating Holdings	42
Searching	45
Cataloging Hints	46
Pitt CONSER Procedures	49
Holdings	50
Relationship to Pitt Internal Records	53
Preservation	53
Statistics	54
Future Changes	55
Conclusion	56

The Newspaper Cataloging Manual and AACR2   59
Jim E. Cole

General Rules	60
Title and Statement of Responsibility Area	61
Edition Area	62
Numeric and/or Other Chronological, or Other Designation Area	63
Publication, Distribution, Etc., Area	63
Physical Description Area	65
Series Area	65
Note Area	65
Conclusion	66

Rethinking National Policy for Cataloging Microform Reproductions   69
Crystal Graham

The Problem for Patrons	71
The Problem for Catalogers	73
The Problem for Union Lists	78
A Solution	81

Newspapers and Their Readers: The United States Newspaper Program's List of Intended Audience Terms   **85**
   James P. Danky

   Appendix I   88
   Appendix II   105

CATALOGING NEWS   107
   Walter M. High, News Editor

   The Library of Congress   108
   American Antiquarian Society   109
   Kentucky Newspaper Project   110
   Pennsylvania Newspaper Project   111
   West Virginia Newspaper Project   112
   Indiana Newspaper Project   112
   Hawaii Newspaper Project   113
   Alabama Newspaper Project   114
   Center for Research Libraries Newspaper Project   115
   Montana Historical Society   116
   Rutgers University   116
   Kansas Newspaper Project   117
   Utah Newspaper Project   118
   State Historical Society of Wisconsin   118

EDITOR

RUTH C. CARTER, *University of Pittsburgh*

EDITORIAL BOARD

ELIZABETH RUTH BAUGHMAN, *Graduate School of Library & Information Science, University of California, Los Angeles*
MICHAEL CARPENTER, *Library Consultant, Los Angeles*
LOIS MAI CHAN, *College of Library & Information Science, University of Kentucky*
JEAN G. COOK, *Iowa State University*
WILLIAM A. GOSLING, *Duke University*
KATHRYN LUTHER HENDERSON, *Graduate School of Library & Information Science, University of Illinois at Urbana-Champaign*
ROBERT M. HIATT, *The Library of Congress*
JOHN R. JAMES, *Dartmouth College Library*
MARTIN D. JOACHIM, *Indiana University*
MARIE A. KASCUS, *Central Connecticut State University*
CHRISTINA McCAWLEY, *West Chester University*
GERARD McKIERNAN, *Carnegie Museum of Natural History*
DICK R. MILLER, *Lane Medical Library, Stanford University*
CAROLYN J. MUELLER, *University of Colorado*
NOLAN F. POPE, *University of Florida*
ELAINE K. RAST, *Northern Illinois University*
JOHN M. SLUK, *University of Pittsburgh*
RICHARD P. SMIRAGLIA, *University of Illinois at Urbana-Champaign*
SUZANNE STRIEDIECK, *Pennsylvania State University*
ARLENE G. TAYLOR, *Graduate Library School, University of Chicago*
NANCY J. WILLIAMSON, *Faculty of Library & Information Science, University of Toronto*

CATALOGING NEWS EDITOR

WALTER M. HIGH, *North Carolina State University*

PRODUCTION EDITOR

MOYRA EVANS

Foreword

The United States Newspaper Program (USNP) constitutes the most geographically extensive and most comprehensive original cataloging enterprise undertaken in this country. Through grant support from the National Endowment for the Humanities, fifty states, the U.S. Trust Territories, and some fifteen national newspaper repositories will enter bibliographic and holdings records into the OCLC/CONSER database for an estimated 300,000 newspaper titles. Well over 15,000 institutions will participate in the program as catalogers crisscross the states to record holdings in public libraries, county courthouses, newspaper offices, college and university libraries, and sometimes in private hands. The end result of the USNP will not only be the vastly enhanced access to newspapers provided by an online database and numerous offline bibliographic products, but also the preservation of hundreds of titles important for research. To this end, cataloging is in service to preservation, for detailed holdings records will furnish information enabling states and institutions to fill gaps and complete runs.

Cooperation and interchange among project participants characterize the effective operation of the program. On the national level, cooperative managerial responsibilities between the Endowment and the Library of Congress were formalized in 1984 through an inter-agency agreement stipulating the respective program roles of the two federal agencies. The Endowment provides overall policy direction and grant management, while as monitor of the CONSER database, the Library of Congress provides quality control over records and furnishes technical advice to the projects.

The program was launched by grants to six repositories with extensive holdings covering the fifty states. The initial six participants included the American Antiquarian Society, the Center for Research Libraries, New York Historical Society, Kansas State Historical Society, the State Historical Society of Wisconsin, and Western Reserve Historical Society. The Library of Congress soon joined the effort as a seventh national repository, though not with Endowment grant funds, since NEH is prohibited from making grants to other federal agencies. Collectively, these repositories were estimated to hold over 50,000 U.S. titles. Entry of their records would allow the database to be built quickly and furnish a large body of bibliographic records to which state projects would add

© 1986 by The Haworth Press, Inc. All rights reserved.

holdings. As it turns out, many of the holdings at the national repositories are either very short runs or single issues. State projects have had to enhance a large number of exisiting records and some anticipated cataloging efficiencies have been lost. Nonetheless, there was an important outcome of the work of the initial repository projects beyond the creation of records.

Cataloging rules for newspapers were only formulated with the advent of the U.S. Newspaper Program, and until their use by the initial national repository projects, the rules existed in a vacuum. Implementation of the rules demanded agreement among project participants on interpretation. To refine the rules became one of the major and most far-reaching tasks of the initial projects, and several special meetings were held at the Library of Congress to arrive at common solutions to cataloging questions. Even before cataloging began, project participants meeting for training at OCLC in January, 1983 discussed the crucial need for subject access to newspapers. They agreed to use the "intended audience" field of the local data record for this purpose and to employ as their subject authority a listing prepared by the State Historical Society of Wisconsin. The group also agreed that the primary point of access to newspapers would be geographic rather than by title. This decision determined the format of OCLC offline products for states and repositories, though not the format of the recently-published *OCLC/USNP National Union List*, which is arranged alphabetically by title, with separate indices for subject or language, place of publication, and dates of publication.

While the major cataloging issues were resolved during the first year of the program's operations, the real test remains with the state projects. It is a relatively easy task to maintain centralized quality control over a few number of record-entry sites, as is the CONSER model. It is far more difficult to develop accurate cataloging records and to maintain quality control over records from on-site cataloging at numerous locations throughout a state, not all of which are environmentally hospitable to cataloging work. These circumstances provide an element of adventure not available in routine cataloging and there are often concomitant rewards, for example, in finding hitherto unrecorded or unknown titles. Nonetheless, the highly dispersed nature of the cataloging, sometimes in a library, sometimes in a barn or attic, places large demands on quality control procedures, and it is to the great credit of the state projects and to the technical coordination provided by the Library of Congress that so much is being done so well.

In that the U.S. Newspaper Program grew out of the desire of historians to have an update of Winifred Gregory's *American Newspapers*, published in 1937, it is natural to think of the program primarily in bibliographic terms. When CONSER was designated as the database for the program, the effort was naturally viewed as a cooperative venture in serials cataloging. There is a major difference, however, between a serials record in CONSER and a USNP record. USNP records contain detailed holdings statements, and it is this union listing component that constitutes the heart of the program. In truth, the U.S. Newspaper Program is a preservation program, making use of bibliographic data to provide the fullest information for preservation purposes. The state and repository projects are creating the nation's most exhaustive union list of titles and holdings in order to select the most important titles and most complete runs for preservation microfilming. From the Endowment's perspective, cataloging is both an end in itself—the provision of access—and a means to an end—the assurance of access for future generations of researchers who will find newspapers one of the most valued resources for the study of American life and culture.

Jeffrey Field
Assistant Director
Office of Preservation
National Endowment for
the Humanities

EDITORIAL

For the past several years I have had the pleasure and privilege of being involved in the Pennsylvania Newspaper Project—one of the many current and future projects within the scope of the United States Newspaper Program (USNP). Everyone I know who is a part of the USNP in any capacity is unbelievably enthusiastic and excited about the Program.

What explains the incredible fascination with the Program? Any number of factors, I suppose. One basic appeal is that the USNP provides an opportunity to participate directly in the process of describing and preserving primary resources in our American heritage. In addition, the state projects have elicited feelings of state pride and created a forum for representatives of many institutions throughout a state to work together for common goals. Still another factor is the enthusiastic support for the program by such institutions and agencies as the National Endowment for the Humanities, the Library of Congress, and OCLC. It is certain this widespread cooperative program could not be so successful without their combined resources and support.

This issue of *Cataloging & Classification Quarterly* presents a broad overview of the cataloging aspects of the United States Newspaper Program. Harold Cannon summarizes the origins of the USNP and reviews the involvements with it of the National Endowment for the Humanities (NEH). He notes that the Newspaper Program is under the auspices of the Office of Preservation of NEH and will serve as a model for other large scale preservation efforts. He stresses the necessity for preservation of the newspapers by microfilming. As most newspaper project catalogers learn rapidly, many newspapers can not be cataloged because they are so brittle that they crumble as they are handled. Consequently, it is necessary that those papers receive preservation microfilming first and cataloging second.

Robert Harriman from the Library of Congress describes the task of coordinating a geographically distributed project and one that is breaking new ground in terms of cataloging newspapers. This has required reaching agreement on a definition of newspapers, developing a newspaper cataloging manual, and making rule interpretations on an almost constant basis in the early stages of the project.

Two articles deal directly with the process of cataloging. Rebecca Wilson and Sue Kellerman from the Pennsylvania State University recount their experiences and procedures in cataloging at a different location nearly every day. The procedures evolved by the Penn State team should be helpful to others about to undertake on-site visits. As Pennsylvania has cataloging distributed among four project sites, an important component of its project is internal quality control procedures. The work at the University of Pittsburgh site which provides CONSER authentication for all newspaper cataloging in Pennsylvania is described by Faye Leibowitz and Cathy Sorensen.

Jim Cole from the Iowa Newspaper Project looks in depth at the differences between the *Newspaper Cataloging Manual* and *AACR2* and the LC Rule interpretations. A second article dealing with descriptive cataloging is Crystal Graham's. She offers suggestions for revising policy regarding cataloging microform reproductions. Her article is included in this issue because the USNP has successfully applied the master record concept urged by Graham.

Subject access for newspapers is dealt with in the article by James Danky in which the actual use to date in USNP records of the intended audience terms is reviewed. The list of intended audience terms authorized for the project is published here as is information on procedures to validate new terms.

The issue concludes with our regular feature: the *Cataloging News* column by Walter High. This issue's News Column provides a description and status report of many of the newspaper projects completed or in progress as of late 1985.

I am very pleased to be able to help in the publication of this issue on the United States Newspaper Program. It is truly a privilege to be a part of such an enormous and significant undertaking and to have the opportunity to share it with others.

Ruth C. Carter
Editor

The National Endowment for the Humanities and the United States Newspaper Program

Harold Cannon

ABSTRACT. The origin of the U.S. Newspaper Program and the involvement with it by the National Endowment for the Humanities are reviewed. Activities of the Endowment's Office of Preservation are described along with the U.S. Newspaper Program's contributions as a model for future cooperative preservation programs.

The importance of newspapers for purposes of historical research is too obvious to require comment, especially before this audience. And it is for the sake of historical researchers that the National Endowment for the Humanities (NEH) became involved in the U.S. Newspaper Program (USNP). The idea for the program grew out of the work of the Committee on Bibliographical and Research Needs of the Organization of American Historians (OAH). Under the chairmanship of the late Walter Rundell, the Committee proposed to the OAH in 1969 that a revision of Winifred Gregory's *American Newspapers, 1821-1936* was badly needed. Shortly thereafter the Endowment asked the American Council of Learned Societies to provide a list of the research tools most needed by scholars in the humanities. A revision of Gregory was high among the priorities of the Organization of American Historians.

With Endowment grant support during 1973 through 1975, the OAH began to plan an update of the Gregory volume. Although the OAH began with the idea that another book would suffice, it soon became apparent that an adequate newspaper reference work would have to contain far more information than had been reported in Gregory.

The OAH soon learned that the core work of a national newspaper program—bibliographic description and union listing—called for library rather than historical expertise. Furthermore, development of the CONSER national serials database and the concurrent development of the

---

Harold Cannon is Director, Office of Preservation, National Endowment for the Humanities, Washington, DC 20506.
This article is based on a talk presented at the Pennsylvania Library Association Annual Conference in October 1985.

MARC-S format suggested that building a national newspaper database would be far superior to any mere revision of Gregory. To incorporate library expertise into the OAH project, the OAH invited the Library of Congress (LC) to become affiliated with the endeavor and Don Wisdom, then Chief of LC's Serial Division, became the Library's chief liaison with the OAH project. A second Endowment grant to the OAH in 1976 was described as the "OAH-Library of Congress United States Newspapers Project." This grant launched the Iowa Pilot Project. I took over the direction of the Divison of Research Programs in the summer of 1976, and so it was at that time that I became involved in the evolution of the USNP.

To test the feasibility of operating in a state, the OAH, with Endowment funds, conducted a pilot project in Iowa during 1977–1978. The project's principal product was a standard bibliography, but in the course of collecting information, many new titles were discovered. This discovery is being repeated in many of the state projects now underway, and it means that our estimate of some 300,000 titles nationwide may be very wide of the mark. It also became clear that a major preservation effort to save these old newspapers was called for, since many of them were literally crumbling away.

During 1978 and 1979 advisory meetings were convened in Washington to sketch out the guidelines for the U.S. Newspaper Program. It was also during this time that Elaine Woods, under a Carnegie Foundation grant to the OAH, completed work on the first draft of the newspaper cataloging manual.

In 1981 the Endowment hired Dr. Pearce Grove to help agency staff complete the planning stage of the program. Dr. Grove had participated in several of the project's advisory meetings and had previously produced a bibliography of New Mexico newspapers.

With the arrival of Pearce Grove, the Endowment concluded negotiations with OCLC and the Library of Congress to provide for CONSER entries by U.S. Newspaper Program participants. Having OCLC/CONSER serve as the host database not only provided the program with an online cataloging facility, but also with a means for long-term updating of the records by the project participants.

The Endowment distributed program guidelines in 1982 and invited six national repositories to submit proposals to begin the program. The Endowment reasoned that, with holdings of from two to seven thousand titles from all states and territories, large repositories would build the database rapidly. To increase the pace of record entry even further, the Library of Congress put a renewed emphasis on cataloging its own collections, thereby becoming a seventh national repository. In addition, the New York State Library, working with Title II-C funds to catalogue its newspaper holdings, agreed to follow the USNP/CONSER procedures and became an eighth national repository.

The next stage was to invite applications from individual states and territories. It was hoped that relevant institutions within a state would agree to one of their number assuming a leadership role in the program and applying to the NEH for a planning grant. Subsequently, for each state and territory, there would be grants made for bibliographic entry into the database and for preservation microfilming. In 1983, through Pearce Grove's enthusiastic marketing of the program, the Endowment made 17 awards, including bibliographic projects for Montana and the Virgin Islands. In 1984 the results of the planning grants were assessed and 6 states were awarded bibliographic implementation grants. In addition, two more states were awarded planning grants. Pennsylvania was among the six states who won both planning and implementation grants in the first two years of the full program. At present, there are 22 states and territories and 8 national repositories involved in planning and implementation activities. In November 1985 the Endowment will make awards for another 3 planning and 4 bibliographic implementation projects.

The Library of Congress and the Endowment agreed to share in the management of the USNP. The specifics of the arrangement are detailed in an Interagency Agreement signed by the Librarian of Congress and the Endowment's Chairman. The arrangement is predicated on both agencies providing a long-term commitment to the program. I might note that the coordination between LC and NEH is an ideal cooperative arrangement, for it would be impossible for NEH to offer the technical guidance that LC's Technical Coordinator provides on a daily basis to the projects.

From the Endowment's standpoint, two issues remain paramount in the management of the projects. These are productivity and preservation. It was impossible for the first repository projects to estimate accurately the rate of cataloging progress, but now that some 35,000 records have been created, we have a much clearer view of what it takes to produce a record and what it takes for a project to come in on time. And, as always, time is money. To date, the Endowment has provided $3.5 million in grant funds. By the end of this calendar year, that figure should increase to $4.4 million. We expect the program to take another twenty years or more to complete, and we are determined to conclude the projects as quickly and economically as possible, without any lowering of standards.

Our second concern is that the program move quickly towards the preservation microfilming of endangered newspapers. The Endowment has placed the USNP within its new Office of Preservation, thereby giving its preservation goals added emphasis. This brief account of the history of the program has shown that preservation was from the first a goal of a national newspaper effort. The 1982 version of the USNP guidelines set out three stages of project activity—planning, cataloging, and preservation. Each stage was to have been completed before the next stage began. A new edition of the guidelines, which will soon be available, will allow a state or national repository to combine bibliographic control and preservation into a single implementation project. This should not only speed along the preservation effort, but also cut costs involved in creating separate bibliographic entries for microfilmed items.

The Endowment's role in the USNP has been most unusual, if not downright uncharacteristic. In every other funding category, the agency is passive and receptive; elsewhere we make no attempt to mandate standards or insist on consistency (we expect all our grants to exemplify excellence, but we recognize that that esteemed abstraction has a thousand different faces). In no other category do we have an agreement with the institution that guarantees quality control in all projects we support. How this came about, and its implications for future policy deserve some notice.

As I have recollected, it was apparent, at least to historians initially, that there was a great need for this resource. The Endowment responded, typically enough, by making a grant to the institution that had identified the need—OAH. That organization soon found that it needed the partnership of the nation's leading research library, and its own role diminished thereafter. That is entirely appropriate: the shipbuilder is no more than a passenger once the ship is launched. Our difficulty with the Library of Congress was that we could not support its newspaper activities, however broad, with grants. LC is a federal agency and gets its funds from the public purse just as we do. But we could jointly administer a national program with each of us performing the functions most appropriate to our mandates. Hence the agreement, and the program. Only similar circumstances could produce such results a second time, and perhaps those similar circumstances are evident now.

One of the ironies of the Endowment's new Office of Preservation—designed, obviously, to preserve much more than just newspapers—is that its great model project is the USNP. I see this as an irony if only because, not so long ago there was no settled definition of a newspaper that satisfied librarians and bibliographers and many repositories (otherwise respectable, I am told) treated newspapers as ephemera. The preservation problem of embrittled books in the nation's libraries is several years behind newspapers, even though we have been able to identify books for many years, and our catalogues of them stretch back to Alexandria. We have nothing like a state-by-state approach to that problem, and we have no single database for books that have been preserved, i.e., microfilmed. Not yet, at least. But, as I have implied, we have the USNP as a model, and the Endowment may well need to be as aggressive again if the cause of preservation for books, journals, manuscripts, documents, maps, drawings, plans, photographs, film, and tapes is to be furthered. Our new guidelines will welcome national, cooperative projects, but this does not mean that we expect them to spring up full-grown like Athena from the head of Zeus. Such projects may well need some exceptional nurture and attention that could exceed our traditional role of simple funding; fortunately our legislative mandate is broad enough to warrant such license.

The Endowment has been making awards for preservation activities since 1979. During the past five years the Endowment has supported projects to train curators in preservation techniques, to survey the extent of the deterioration of scholarly resources, to support cooperative and selective microfilming efforts, and to effect improvements in preservation technology. The FY 1985 budget request announced a new Endowment initiative in this arena and the formation of a separate Office of Preservation.

The raw materials of scholarship in the humanities are the documents housed in libraries, archives, museums, and other repositories. No matter how carefully these essential resources have been maintained, the inherent instability of much of this documentation guarantees that its present condition is grossly deteriorated.

Records on paper, whether print or manuscript, furnish the most devastating evidence of decay. The introduction of unpurified wood-pulp as a base for paper and the adoption of alum-rosin sizing in the 1860s have caused the "brittle book" problem in the nation's libraries. Surveys have shown that 25–30 percent of the volumes at the Library of Congress and at the university libraries of Stanford and Yale are so deteriorated that they cannot be handled without suffering further damage.

Most of these volumes were published in the period 1870–1920—a period that witnessed the rise of the graduate schools in this country and the first flowerings of American post-doctoral scholarship. Books endure better in cold, damp surroundings; the inadequate or non-existent heating systems of many older libraries of Europe have provided legendary discomfort for scholars for centuries and their collections are in better condition for it. This is therefore a peculiarly American problem, but, although urgency may not be as great elsewhere, it is also an international concern; for example, the British Library recently announced formation of a preservation office.

More than 95 percent of American scholarly books are now published on acid-free paper, and most research libraries are likely to adopt some kind of de-acidification process for new or nearly-new books, following the model of the Library of Congress. The future looks much better than the past, and it is retrospective action that is most needed now.

Since de-acidification stabilizes the condition of a book, the only recourse with a volume in an advanced state of deterioration is to copy it. Microfilming continues to be the preferred technology for this reformatting process; the optical disc is still at an experimental stage and cannot be guaranteed to endure more than ten years, although it can be duplicated inexpensively.

It is important now to increase the productivity of selective microfilming and to guarantee national access to materials that have been preserved. At present some 100,000 volumes are being filmed annually. Individual institutions are doing much of this work; in most cases the information about the filming is not being filmed annually. Individual institutions are doing much of this work; in most cases the information about the filming is not being shared through a national database. Information about national efforts of this kind is being gathered by the Council on Library Resources, which has formed a Committee on Preservation and Access.

The Endowment is beginning to play a leadership role by publicizing this program nationally, bringing together different kinds of institutions to further this work, and encouraging private sector contributions through matching grants. Over time, we should aim at increasing national microfilming efforts to a new annual total of 200,000, with all titles entered into a national database so that access is virtually guaranteed throughout the country. Microfilming a 300-page volume and completing the bibliographic entry for it costs about $60. A copy of the film thereafter costs $2 or $3.

Since only some 5 percent of what is at risk could be saved in this way, (twenty years at the rate of 200,000 volumes annually would save 4 million of the 75 million books presently at risk), it is obvious that selection is a vitally important step in this process. So far three approaches to this difficult problem have evolved: (1) user-demand at individual institutions alerts librarians to the condition of particular volumes, which may then be cued for microfilming; (2) research collections of unique and established importance to scholarship may be microfilmed selectively according to common general priorities—this is the approach employed in the cooperative microfilming project administered by the Research Libraries Group at nine leading research libraries and funded by the Endowment and the Mellon Foundation; and (3) scholars in a particular discipline could review bibliographies and determine what has highest priority for preservation—a grant to the American Philological Association is currently supporting a project of this type for books in the field of classics. In addition to these three methods of approaching preservation, the Endowment has announced a priority in this program for materials relating to the cultural, intellectual, and literary history of the United States.

The confidence that the Endowment can succeed in this necessarily cooperative venture is based on our experience with the U.S. Newspaper Program.

Projects supported by the Office of Preservation are of two kinds: (1)

projects concerned with preservation training, microfilming, planning and surveying, regional conservation services, and institutional programs, and (2) the awards to individual states and territories to facilitate their participation in the United States Newspaper Program. The USNP is a model—so far the only one—of the kind of cooperative preservation activity we hope to encourage for other materials. This distinction, therefore, is not a difference in kind but in degree of development.

I should like to end by mentioning with pride the publication earlier this summer of the first National Union List of Newspapers issued in eight paperback volumes and in microfiche by the Online Computer Library Center of Dublin, Ohio. This alphabetized list of the 35,000 titles already entered in the CONSER database is complemented by three indices: date, place, and intended audience and language and will be updated annually. This is the first tangible product of the USNP, and I plan to share it with the members of the National Council for the Humanities when they meet in Washington November 7th and 8th, 1985. I know they will be as pleased as I am with these first fruits of the Endowment's many investments in this program.

Coordination of Cataloging Practices in the United States Newspaper Program

Robert B. Harriman, Jr.

ABSTRACT. The bibliographic component of the United States Newspaper Program comprises cooperative efforts to locate and catalog the more than 300,000 newspapers published in the U.S. and its territories since colonial times, and to enter bibliographic and holdings information about those titles into the CONSER data base. The attempt to gain bibliographic control over existing newspaper collections, as well as the attempt to gather and organize previously uncollected materials, has required procedural adaptations determined by a unique set of working conditions. The scale of the program has required specificity of goals and objectives, satisfying standards for inclusion of records in the national serials data base while maintaining reasonable economies. This paper outlines some of the mechanisms put in place to achieve that balance.

The goal of the United States Newspaper Program (USNP) is the provision of access and selective preservation of the content of newspapers published in the United States and its territories since colonial times. To accomplish this goal, the cooperative efforts of hundreds of librarians, archivists, preservation experts, historians, and journalists are required to locate and catalog the more than 300,000 newspaper titles that are estimated to be held by libraries, historical societies, archives, courthouses, publishers, and private collectors all over the United States, and to preserve by microfilming those titles deemed most important for research.

Since 1973 the National Endowment for the Humanities (NEH) has helped support efforts to provide access to newspaper collections. Since that time, as well, the Library of Congress has provided support and expertise to those efforts and has continued publication of *Newspapers in Microform*[1] (NIM), first published in 1948. In recent years, the emergence of a national plan to gain bibliographic control over newspapers has brought these two federal agencies and, through the CONSER (CONversion of SERials) Project, the Online Computer Library Center (OCLC) as host utility, into close cooperation in guiding and directing activities

---

Robert B. Harriman, Jr., Technical Coordinator, U.S. Newspaper Program, Serial Record Division, Library of Congress.

© 1986 by The Haworth Press, Inc. All rights reserved.

toward the achievement of the program's goal. Over the next decade, the Endowment will support projects in all fifty states plus six U.S. Territories and the District of Columbia. In addition, projects will be supported in several institutions whose collections are of significant size and scope and represent unique holdings.

The U.S. Newspaper Program is an undertaking on a grand scale, and would be an exciting challenge on that basis alone. Even if we could imagine a much more perfect world than that in which we find ourselves, a world in which librarians had collected newspapers and organized those collections as conscientiously as even, say, government publications, the effort to convert cataloging data to machine-readable form and to organize holdings and location information to serve preservation and acquisition requirements would be massive.

The real world, however, doesn't even come close to that. Newspapers have suffered relative neglect in the hands of libraries and librarians, a fact even more troubling when one considers the expense of handling, storage, maintenance and other associated costs that will be consumed by any newspaper collection. When collection management and maintenance costs will inevitably be high, one wonders that so little effort has been made to provide better bibliographic control and thus relieve subsequent expenses.

STATUS OF BIBLIOGRAPHIC CONTROL

The justifications most often offered for the neglect of newspaper collections have to do with the physical bulk of the items and with the fragility of newsprint, both characteristics presenting multiple problems to those wishing to handle these materials in any systematic way, much less organize them for easy access. The latter problem, the fragility of the paper itself, is particularly characteristic of newspapers published since the turn of the century, when the use of highly acidic wood pulp newsprint became general throughout the United States. Newspapers published in the 1800's and earlier are more likely to survive over time due to the use of cotton rag paper.

Many of the earliest newspapers published in the United States can be (carefully) read in their original form. Even these titles, though, have been collected more often than not as souvenirs, only a few issues of a run obtained as representative, often bound in collections organized by chronology or by association with an historic event.

Rarely have libraries been able to commit resources to collecting and maintaining complete runs of these early papers. In fact, some libraries are actually contributing to the future impossibility of obtaining such complete runs by purchasing individual issues from dealers who can obtain greater profit by breaking up the runs than by holding out for the rare buyer who can afford the entire run. Our attention was recently drawn to the catalog of a Connecticut mail-order house offer "actual complete American newspapers from the 1700's and 1800's." As a catalog "exclusive," complete with a "certificate of authenticity," the issues sold as: Pre-1800—$45.00; 1800–1861—$20.00; Civil War Years—$20.00; and so on. It will be obvious to anyone involved in newspaper acquisition that the best "headlines," which can demand several thousand dollars an issue, have been culled from this offering.

Less subject to verification, but probably as much a factor for neglect as the material and physical problems newspapers pose, is the implication that the materials are by their very nature—with the exceptions, of course, of those "headline" issues—ephemeral. In many libraries, one even gets the impression that a better sort of person would read such things in the privacy of their own home or club, but certainly not in the same rooms where real books are being read.

There are glaring exceptions, which thus prove the rule. In many states, law requires that certain newspapers be collected and held as documents of public record by county and state agencies or archives. When that designated agency has been the state library, treatment of newspapers has been most like that of other library materials. County courthouses and clerks' offices, on the other hand, have found themselves ill equipped to confront the problems of storage, organization and access that compliance with the law would imply.

Newspaper publishers have traditionally maintained a complete bound file of their publication, and microfilming arrangements now allow economy of storage and access and thus encourage the maintaining of a complete backfile. Time and time again, though, we hear the story of the flood or fire that destroyed the bound backfile.

Just as some institutions have benefited through association with collectors of varied whim, and thus received as the legacies of those collectors riches of the exotic and occasionally erotic, several institutions now serve as custodians of fine and comprehensive newspaper collections. Most of those same institutions service and maintain those collections excellently. In every case, though, the attendent difficulty and expense of handling have argued against the assignment of a higher relative priority to the processing of newspapers. If time is to be assigned and money to be spent, goes the imagined argument, wouldn't such resources be better utilized in dealing with materials that are more . . . permanent?

At the Library of Congress, cataloging of newpapers began only in the late 1970's. The Library of Congress' newspaper collection, housed in and maintained by the Serial and Government Publications Division, totals more than 35,000 titles, of which approximately 13,000 are U.S.

publications. The count of individual pieces—individual bound volumes, microfilm reels, loose issues, etc.—totals approximately 2,200,000 pieces. In microfilm holdings alone, the collection includes 370,000 reels of film. The Library currently receives 1600 newspaper titles, of which 600 are U.S. publications. Obviously, the Library of Congress can collect only those newspapers from the larger cities in the U.S. and throughout the world, titles judged to be most important to the researchers who use our collections. The collection and custody of local and regional newspapers, as mentioned above, has traditionally been the role of state or county agencies.

In 1976, as a result of early discussion which would lead to the development of what we now know as the United States Newspaper Program, the Library of Congress began to catalog its collection of U.S. newspapers and to enter those catalog records into the CONSER database. The initial effort was carried out with very limited staff resources, and only recently has the Library been able to assign an appropriate number of catalogers to this undertaking. Even with this late start, our experience has shown that LC was steps ahead of many libraries in attempting to bring its newspaper collections under bibliographic control.

The Library of Congress' interest and activity in the bibliographic control of newspapers have extended beyond the boundaries of our own collection for many years. Since its publication in 1948, librarians and researchers have depended upon NIM as a principle source of information about newspaper resources in North American libraries. While limited by design and intent to providing information only about newspapers in reproduction, NIM has served a de facto role as the only current national union list of newspapers. Clarence Brigham's *History and Bibliography of American Newspapers, 1690–1820,*[2] and Winifred Gregory's *American Newspapers, 1821–1936,*[3] have been the only other bibliographies national in scope, but, obviously, cannot be considered timely. Each of these publications exhibits limitations and inaccuracies inherent to the particular survey method employed, and, of course, there is little relationship between current cataloging rules and the description and organization these publications employ.

Beyond the purported inadequacies and inaccuracies or existing bibliographic tools, though, is the fact that these report only what has been collected and brought under at least the most basic level of bibliographic control. And for a great number of these reported titles, as mentioned above, actual holdings are only scattered issues. Clearly, the rest was not lost altogether, just stuck away somewhere. As the program developed, it became clear that the best way to discover what had been published was to go out and find as much as possible, using whatever resources were available to provide clues. The (awful) truth is that most of the newspapers published in the United States remain—in the sense in which librarians understand the term—uncollected . . . out of control.

SUITABLE CLOTHING REQUIRED

In Moundsville, West Virginia, USNP project catalogers were led to a room under the roof of the building which houses the offices of the *Moundsville Daily Echo*. There, stored in fertilizer sacks to provide some protection from the elements, were newspapers collected on the editor's travels around the world and more complete collections, though suffering from storage conditions, of papers published closer to home. In north-central Pennsylvania, catalogers from Pennsylvania State University climbed an extension ladder into a garage attic and found, among the stacks of newspapers stored there, a number of previously undocumented titles. In yet another attic, this time in an abandoned farmhouse in Iowa, catalogers were led to a hoard of nineteenth-century newspapers that had been left to the birds and the weather. Among the mess they found several titles for which they had found references but, prior to that day, no extant copies.

And the discoveries aren't limited to the "field." Project staff at the Indiana State Library judge that during their inventory they discovered the collection to be at least one-third larger than earlier counts indicated— and not merely on the basis of successive entry. A similar revision of collection totals followed the inventory of the newspaper holdings of the Kansas State Historical Society.

HOW YA GONNA KEEP 'EM DOWN IN TECH SERVICES . . .

The work is different. We can show you the photograph of a cataloger sharing desk space (actually, workbench space) with paint cans and power tools and varnish remover. She's cataloging newspapers, in conditions that put the fragility of the material in a whole new context. Available light in attics and basements is rarely sufficient, so we've learned to include supplemental light sources like flashlights and electric lanterns on the list of equipment needed to outfit a cataloger for the field.

The job requires some special qualities. Even in the best cases, where the cataloger has bound volumes to work with, those volumes are too often stored flat on a shelf that's just out of reach. More often than expected, there are "a bunch of old newspapers up over the barn there." A fear of height (or depth, or close quarters) would be a definite handicap. Catalogers doing field work have learned to be a little more curious than might be expected. They've found it's worth it to go so far as to snoop around a bit, get their noses under tables and behind bookcases and into back rooms. Having chanced upon local treasures more than once when doing this, they find it hard to leave a town clerk's office or local historical society without at least giving that back room one more look.

There are hazards, large and small. Too often, there's clear evidence that one or another sort of critter has been seeking food and shelter where others find the contents of history, and sometimes there's the prickly feeling that those critters are still close by and curious about who's messing around in their nest. Sometimes it's best just to get arrangements made right there for transport back to home base where the stuff can be run through the Vacudyne a few times before you feel prepared to handle it. Everyone has limits. And always there's dust, terrible huge quantities of dust. But you don't dare sneeze, for fear of blowing it all away. You get a real sense for what it means to take care.

But that's balanced by the papers themselves. One doesn't have to work with these very long to begin to feel the rhythms of day-to-day activity, to trace the lines of continuity, and to recognize the small gestures and forms of community. Like all good catalogers, we try not to get too distracted by the contents of the materials we're describing, understanding that it's our job just to get these things organized. But one will glance at an article that seems to stand out, and understand suddenly what incredible source material newspapers represent. And a moment later, the town clerk or newspaper publisher or historical society curator will glance over your shoulder and, seeing that same article, will tell you what happened next and who got real mad because of it and that's why that window behind the pulpit has been boarded over ever since.

Catalogers will open a portfolio and find nothing but dust, they'll reach to turn a page that appears to be intact and it comes apart in their hands, and they understand that what's being lost at the moment is not the paper, not the artefact, but those "social" notices and local sports stories and obituaries and school menus that serve as the record of a people going about their daily life. And it goes well beyond simply charming when, among those seemingly "local" news notes is primary source material on the leader of the suffrage movement in Montana or prohibition in Indiana or the mineworkers' union in Pennsylvania. So, when catalogers are working in the back room of the local history society and an older gentleman comes in to say he heard they were going to be in town and remembered his grandfather had left a trunk full of old newspapers that have been in the attic for forty years or more now . . . maybe they'd like to have a look at them? You bet they would.

GETTING ORGANIZED

The task, then, is to gain bibliographic control over a body of material—a bibliographic entity, if you prefer that terminology—that is widely dispersed, even essentially uncollected, and at risk of disappearing altogether. The objectives are to locate the material, provide descriptive and holdings information in machine-readable form to allow broad access to the material, evaluate the physical condition of the material and assess its value for research, identify the most complete files of each title and provide access to those files through interlibrary loan arrangements or direct acquisition, and preserve by microfilming those files deemed most important for research.

The first and most obvious step, and one that was not without pitfall, was to arrive at an accepted definition of the term 'newspaper'. The definition agreed upon[4] by program planners and participants is one that is designed to be as inclusive as it is possible to be of the range of publications that might be considered while still *defining*, i.e., remaining exclusive. Criteria of format, content, and readership are equally considered when evaluating a publication for inclusion within the scope of program coverage.

In attempting to set out guidelines for identification and description of newspapers the assumption was and continues to be that rules for the description of serial publications are sufficient and appropriate for the description of newspapers. Following that assumption, work was begun in the late 1970's to prepare a set of cataloging guidelines and, for conversion, MARC Serials editing conventions, to allow consistent application of rules and procedures in newspaper cataloging activities associated with the USNP. The manual,[5] prepared by Elaine Woods, was completed in 1981. With a working manual completed, the cooperating parties were free to move ahead with the testing of documentation and procedures in selected cataloging sites. Final agreement came also in 1981 allowing entry of USNP records onto the CONSER data base.

As stated above, the Library of Congress had begun cataloging its own collection of U.S. newspapers and was adding those records to the CONSER data base. In order to provide a controlled test of documentation and procedures, and to create a "core" data base on which subsequent state projects could build, the decision was made to identify a group of what were to be called 'repository' projects, institutions whose collections were of significant size and national in scope. These institutions, whose collections were already subject to at least minimal bibliographic control, could create that core data base and could help to establish cataloging standards and procedures to be followed by all subsequent participants.

In fiscal year 1982 the National Endowment for the Humanities awarded grants to the American Antiquarian Society, the Center for Research Libraries, the Kansas State Historical Society, the New York Historical Society, the State Historical Society of Wisconsin, and the Western Reserve Historical Society. Initial estimates predicted that these institutions and the Library of Congress would create a core data base of more than 35,000 bibliographic records, approximately ten percent of the estimated national total.

Through an interagency agreement between the two federal agencies, the Library of Congress is charged with the technical management of the United States Newspaper Program. Through this arrangement, consultation and assistance is provided to projects from the point at which work plans are being drafted to completion of the project. Staff from LC and OCLC develop and implement training programs for cataloging staff, and monitor cataloging and union listing activity throughout the term of the project, ensuring adherence to appropriate standards and procedures.

It was clear to CONSER staff at LC that the increased cataloging and imput activity by USNP projects would require revision of procedures for CONSER "authentication." Prior to USNP, bibliographic records for serials were created on OCLC by CONSER participant libraries and a surrogate of the chief source of information on which the record was based was forwarded to the appropriate Center of Responsibility (LC for U.S. and non-Canadian foreign publications, the National Library of Canada for Canadian-imprint publications). CONSER cataloging staff at the Center of Responsibility reviewed the record for content of description and authoritativeness of headings, and added authentication codes to the record on completion of that review. Those authentication codes, in turn, triggered selection of the record for distribution on the MARC Distribution Service-Serials tape. This process of review was a time-consuming activity and posed several serious barriers to allowing distribution of newspaper records, not the least of which was the problem of delivery of suitable surrogates of newspapers to the Library of Congress.

Fortunately, an alternative to this plan of work was already being considered for CONSER cataloging. The alternative proposal involved the decentralization of the authentication procedure, allowing the inputting agency to authenticate the descriptive portion of the record, thus allowing more timely distribution of the cataloging data. The authentication code appearing in the record would inform users of the level of authentication.

This alternative was adopted into the plan of work for USNP participants, who use the authentication agency code *msc* in the records they create. This code was originally defined as Library of Congress minimal level cataloging, but has been redefined to reflect the authoritativeness of the headings in the record. The code *msc* is now used in any

CONSER authenticated record in which one or more name heading may not be authoritative. This step accomplished, the way was cleared to incorporate USNP cataloging into the CONSER Project.

Cataloging staff from the six projects were brought to OCLC's headquarters in Dublin, Ohio in January, 1983, for a five-day workshop conducted by LC and OCLC staff. This first workshop functioned both to provide training in CONSER cataloging procedures and to serve as a forum for the development of new procedures specific to the unique cataloging and union listing activities to be carried out in the USNP. Practicum sessions allowed testing of the manuals and documentation that had been developed to that date, and significant revision and review was accomplished during the week. Of equal, if not greater, benefit was the establishment of the cooperative working structure that would be required to accomplish initial program goals.

MAKING IT WORK

Perhaps the most significant departure from accepted cataloging practice necessary for the success of the USNP cataloging projects was the adoption of a "master" record approach to recording holdings of newspapers on microform. Conventional practice would call for a separate entry to be made when a library has newspaper holdings in more than one physical medium. Also, when holdings are in reproduction, a separate record would be made when the publisher of that reproduction changes. In an online cooperative file, this creates a situation bordering in some cases on chaos. The most serious problem for the USNP work plan was the bibliographic confusion encountered when trying to trace a single newspaper chronologically through its history and linking relationships, and trying to make sense of holdings at the same time. Further problems relating to eventual size of the file, searching time, update problems, and serious barriers to coherent output all argued against acceptance of conventional practice.

The alternative convention adopted for the United States Newspaper Program calls for the creation of a single bibliographic record describing the newspaper as originally published, i.e., on newsprint. Individual holdings records are created, utilizing OCLC's union list subsystem, for each distinct format held by participant institutions. Thus, rather than having to create multiple bibliographic records to represent local holdings of a run of one title, portions of which have been filmed by separate producers, as well as another separate record for local holdings of the original, participants can organize their holdings by format and institution in relation to a single bibliographic description. While this approach sacrifices detailed description of the microfilm publication, it allows access to holdings more directly and efficiently than would be possible following conventional practice for the cataloging of microforms. It should be noted here that the information that is lost is information that would most logically be of use to acquisitions librarians (since a separate local holdings record will be created for master microforms, preservation interests are served by USNP procedures). In a program such as this, where resource sharing is being facilitated by participant cataloging and union listing activities, and where the majority of materials are of interest within given regions, it is felt that the acquisitions component is served efficiently by the master record approach.

Participants in the first cataloging workshop also developed a device for providing access to those newspapers published for a specific ethnic or special interest group. Facing opposition at the time to the identification within the bibliographic record itself of data elements defining ethnic or religious groups, USNP workshop participants agreed to record such information in the local data record. A thesaurus of terms was created[6] for the use of program participants, and OCLC staff identified and provided off-line indexing capability of a new subfield to accommodate this information. A field providing access to the geographic target of the newspaper was defined for the serials format in 1981. Thus, two of the major access points most useful to researchers, geographic and ethnic or special interest group, while not indexed for online searching, were available as index options in off-line products.

As a result of work carried out during the first workshop, and continuing revision and review during the first year of the program, work began on a new edition of the Manual. In the spring of 1984, the *Newspaper Cataloging Manual*; CONSER/USNP Edition,[7] was published. The revised manual incorporated rule revisions and interpretations issued since publication of the earlier manual, as well as examples drawn from work done by the repository projects.

As specific program needs arise that require consensus for resolution, an ad hoc committee, designated as the USNP Technical Procedures Committee, is called together to study the alternatives and make recommendations. Technical management staff at LC monitor the need for rule interpretations, system enhancements and modifications, etc., and work with appropriate agencies to accomplish those. USNP staff at LC and at OCLC are in close contact with the program administrators in the Office of Preservation of the National Endowment for the Humanities to facilitate the ongoing administration of the program and to monitor progress of the long range plan for carrying out and completing the program.

The primary cataloging concern arising out of the first year of USNP activity was the level of description appropriate to the building of a national data base and union list of holdings, particularly when that cataloging is based on incomplete and often scattered holdings. Until the state projects began their work, this concern was also the most difficult to communicate to participants.

Ideally, when one catalogs retrospectively a serial publication, the entire run of that publication is available to the cataloger. When that is not the case, as the rules state, one bases the description on the earliest issue available. A normal working assumption, though, when one is cataloging retrospectively, is that the cataloger is working with the best information available. When holdings are slight, the description is often "filled out"—linking information supplied, dates of beginning and cessation of publication provided—with reference to secondary sources. In the most careful cataloging departments, this research is extensive and is extensively documented in the record itself through repeated citation of sources used.

The state project design of the United States Newspaper Program should allow cataloging to be done in conditions as close to the ideal as possible. State projects are not limited to only institutional holdings; in fact the key to the success of a project is the quality and comprehensiveness of the inventory in seeking out and working with the newspapers themselves, rather than relying on previous work. When the vast majority of newspapers published in the United States are local in character and coverage, it should come as no surprise to us to discover that the most complete holdings will be found closest to home—with the understanding that they may be found in the courthouse basement, or someone's barn, rather than in a library. Thus the need for reliance on secondary source materials to "fill out" the descriptive record should be minimal. Rather, these sources are used appropriately in providing preliminary inventory information and in providing extra "clues" to the cataloger attempting to solve bibliographic problems.

Thus, while individual institutions were being given more authority on the one hand, in that they were "self-authenticating" records on a national data base, they were also being asked to temper that authority somewhat. The amount of effort dedicated to cataloging a newspaper, they began to understand should be appropriate to the extent of their actual holdings of that newspaper. Only when one knows a great deal about the entire run of a given title is one fully justified in creating an extensive descriptive record for that title. Reliance on secondary sources to "fill out" a record is discouraged. Rather, catalogers are instructed to use secondary sources as they are designed to be used, i.e., as research tools to lead one to primary source information.

Newspaper publishers in the United States are paradigms of fierce independence and the tendency to be "creative," so it should be no surprise that they cared little for the sorts of consistent behavior—like not messing around with the title—that serials librarians consider to be indices of civilization. Words appear and disappear on newspaper mastheads with alarming unpredictability; mergers occur that combine names and numbering schemes that multiply over the years, by which time the publisher, struck down in the road by a fit of historical consciousness, returns pious and repentant to the name and numbering system that started it all a hundred years ago. Special occasions, as they often do today, mean special graphic treatment, like dressing up the masthead with flags and stars and various of the pantheon. And on those most historic occasions, what better acknowledgement than to return for a day to the paper that existed when we were all riding scooters? My local paper does all these things. It's only one of the reasons that cataloging from your collection of Centennial or Exposition or Armistice issues is a chancy business and suspiciously monographic in result.

Faced with these limitations, catalogers in the initial projects began to alter their understanding of the role of individual institutions in a cooperative cataloging project. When holdings were neither complete nor unique, it was probable that not only the data base as a whole but also individual records for a title or for the several titles in a run were being pieced together by catalogers at more than one institution. While this particular phenomenon will diminish somewhat as the program becomes more state project oriented, and thus materials are less likely to be held by more than one institution, it has been a dominant factor in work to this point.

Both in an attempt to avoid the hazard of "over-cataloging" and to establish a minimum threshold of acceptability, the USNP base level record was outlined. The record outline specifies the minimum data element set necessary for access and for unambiguous identification of a newspaper. Bibliographic records constructed according to these guidelines, and based solely on the issues in hand, serve as the bibliographic core data to which enhancement can be made as appropriate. Since the base level record is the primary identifier, it is also used as the basis for determining cataloging costs, thus allowing for some equality of funding when project scope and resources differ greatly.

At the time cataloging and input activity for USNP began, discussion of the accepted standard practice for recording holdings and location information was still far from concluded. Thus, the form of notation and the conventions adopted at the time were based on the best guess of what the eventual standard might look like. Agreement on the standard[8] and publication of the *USMARC Format For Holdings and Locations*[9] has precipitated review of USNP procedures and documentation outlining revised procedures is currently in preparation.

FOLLOWING THROUGH

The emergence of preservation concerns as high-priority budget and agenda items in libraries around the world is not due simply to the fact that these concerns are next on the list. Rather, the sustained efforts of a few leaders in the field over the past decade have brought about developments in technology and the sharing of expertise required to administer preservation activities effectively and economically. Simply put, major efforts can now be directed to the task because the success of those efforts is now possible. And, as cooperative efforts like the United States Newspaper Program proceed, the body of data on which future decisions and developments will be made should grow rapidly.

In many ways, the United States Newspaper Program is being asked to serve both as model for cooperative preservation programs and as a laboratory to test methods and procedures crucial to the success of such programs. Even at this early stage, the sharing of ideas and experience among projects has been of measurable benefit, and each new project is more efficiently organized. The organization of projects by state, while perhaps more logical when concentrating on newspapers than on other types of materials, has laid the groundwork of inter-agency cooperation and communication within those states that can be built upon in the future.

Because of the unique character of the United States Newspaper Program, that is, its focus on a body of material that has been less subject to bibliographic control in the past, and the goal of the program being the preservation of the content of that material, management of the cataloging component of the program requires the clear definition of what we are cataloging *for*, what our objectives are in relation to overall program goals.

Cataloging done by participants in the U.S. Newspaper Program will be asked to meet needs relating to the establishment of preservation and acquisitions priorities for state projects and, in some cases, for larger research libraries. The knowledge that a title has been filmed allows available funding to be spent on yet another title. That same cataloging will be asked to serve, as Gregory and Brigham have served, as a source for research on the history of newspapers and newspaper publishing in the United States. Finally, that cataloging will be shared by many individual libraries who will use the records in their own catalogs.

Realistically, the expected result of cataloging activity in the U.S. Newspaper Program should be a solid foundation of bibliographic information about newspapers *on which to build*. Our intent is to satisfy those needs relating to preservation as fully as possible, and at the same time provide accurate and unambiguous descriptive information to meet the needs of libraries and researchers. We are not, however, doing newspaper history. Nor do we expect our cataloging to meet all local needs. What we are providing is data that will make it more possible to do those publishing histories and descriptive information that can be enhanced locally to meet local needs.

The funding provided by the National Endowment for the Humanities to locate, catalog, and selectively preserve the more than 300,000 newspapers published in the United States both meets an immediate need of researchers and provides an opportunity to libraries, research institutions, bibliographic networks, and state and local repositories. I think it is clear to all that, without this funding and support, access to newspapers would remain a problem in most libraries and newspaper preservation efforts would continue to be carried out with only minimal collaboration. Thus even those resources dedicated to the task would be utilized inefficiently, and the loss of a significant body of materials would be inevitable. If the United States Newspaper Program is successful in meeting its goals, then that immediate need of the research community is met. Moreover, by meeting that need, by bringing control and organization to newspaper resources, we will have established the capability to maintain access to those resources. The magnitude of effort required to obtain that capability should convince us all of our responsibility to provide that maintenance, as well as to develop more effective and efficient ways of doing so.

The documentation and standards developed by the Library of Congress and the training provided to program participants are intended to establish that same capability; these are the tools with which work can be continued. What has been exceptional, that is, established procedures for control and access to newspapers, should become commonplace as expertise is shared.

Thus a financial and technical margin of possibility is established, not simply to accomplish the immediate tasks, but also to expand the cooperative relationships to meet other shared needs, to use the skills and experience gained to solve other problems. The rewards of association with this program are in being a part of an effective cooperative effort; in watching collaborative attitudes and mechanisms develop; and in seeing the leadership emerge to achieve the goals and objectives of this program and of the similar efforts that will be required to save our collections.

NOTES

1. *Newspapers in Microform: United States, 1948–1983.* (Washington: Library of Congress, 1972–1984), and *Newspapers in Microform: Foreign Countries, 1948–1983.* (Washington: Library of Congress, 1972–1984).

2. Brigham, Clarence S. *History and Bibliography of American Newspapers, 1690–1820.* (Westport, Conn.: Greenwood Press, 1976, c1975).

3. Gregory, Winifred, ed. *American Newspapers, 1821–1936; a union list of files available in the United States and Canada.* (New York: H. W. Wilson, 1937).

4. The definition adopted is that used by the Library of Congress and adopted for use for NISO (Z39.39), "Compiling Newspaper and Periodical Publishing Statistics" 1979.

5. Woods, Elaine W. *Newspaper Cataloging Manual.* (Washington: Library of Congress, 1981).

6. A list of intended audience terms developed and maintained at the State Historical Society of Wisconsin was adopted for use by the original USNP projects. The list is revised periodically, and it is expected that it will be reissued early in 1986.

7. Harriman, Robert B. *Newspaper Cataloging Manual.* CONSER/USNP Ed. (Washington: Library of Congress, 1984).

8. At this writing, the "American National Standard for Serial Holdings Statements, (Z39.44)" has not been published, and is circulated only in final draft form.

9. *USMARC Format for Holdings and Locations.* (Washington: Library of Congress, 1984).

Challenges of On-Site Cataloging

Rebecca A. Wilson
Lydia Suzanne Kellerman

ABSTRACT. On-site newspaper cataloging in libraries, historical societies, newspaper publishers' offices and private collectors' homes in rural northcentral Pennsylvania created a host of challenges and rewards for project librarians of the Pennsylvania Newspaper Project. The experiences of the Penn State team in their quest to identify, inventory and catalog newspapers in a variety of unorthodox and exciting situations are shared in this article. The paper focuses on problems associated with identifying titles, linking titles, updating cataloging and gathering holdings data, and offers some solutions to those problems.

INTRODUCTION

The publisher led us to a 20-foot ladder. "Up there are the newspapers," he said, pointing to a loft high above the pressroom. "Are you sure you need to examine them all? We do have a list of what's up there." Experience had taught us to assume nothing and to check everything. "Yes, we do need to examine them all," we replied. With workforms, blank local data records, pencils, tape measure and gloves, we climbed the ladder.

The portable lights the pressmen had rigged hung from the rafters and lit the cramped storage area. What we saw was discouraging—even overwhelming. Stacks of bound volumes, laden with dust, thrown carelessly in heaps, were piled to the ceiling. We crawled through the debris to position ourselves among the volumes, and began our work.

And so began a typical on-site visit for the Pennsylvania State University's National Newspaper Project librarians.

Mrs. Wilson and Ms. Kellerman are project librarians for the northcentral portion of the Pennsylvania Newspaper Project, headquartered at The Pennsylvania State University Library. Mrs. Wilson holds a BA in English Literature and Spanish, and an MLS. Ms. Kellerman holds a BA in American Studies and an MLS. Mailing address: W308 Pattee Library The Pennsylvania State University, University Park, PA 16802. Mrs. Wilson's home address: P. O. Box 14, Huntingdon, PA 16652. Ms. Kellerman's home address: 118 Apollo Avenue, Boalsburg, PA 16827. The authors extend gratitude to Dr. Barbara Smith and Suzanne Striedieck for their suggestions and comments on earlier drafts.

BACKGROUND

Penn State's project librarians were assigned the task of identifying, inventorying, and cataloging newspapers in fifteen rural counties in northcentral Pennsylvania, as part of a statewide effort to catalog 9,500 newspapers that were published in the state since 1719.

The rural nature of northcentral Pennsylvania, coupled with its sparse population and lack of major institutions with extensive newspaper holdings, forced the project librarians to rely on visits to many sites to locate the maximum number of newspapers. It was estimated that over 250 sites covering approximately 10,000 miles would be visited in a seventeen-month period.

Having to rely on visits to all types of institutions, i.e., academic, public and school libraries, historical societies, newspaper publishers, and private collectors, created its own problems as well as rewards in attempting to gather the necessary data. Some six months of field work covering over 3000 miles of travel in seven counties, visiting approximately 90 sites, and the experience involved therein is recounted below emphasizing *gathering* the data used for descriptive cataloging for the project.

Although project librarians were hired in separate capacities (one a field librarian, the other a project cataloger), the librarians agreed to share all aspects of the project from the beginning, thus enabling both team members to become thoroughly familiar with the institutions and individuals to be visited, as well as the newspaper titles to be found.

It proved to be a wise decision. Having both librarians on-site enabled the team to do in one day what it would have taken a single person two days to do. The team is also convinced that the massive amounts of data collected on any county visit were more accurately accumulated by having two people focusing on the task, one concentrating on cataloging a title fully, the other on gathering the holdings data and the condition reports.

PRE-SITE VISIT PREPARATIONS

Prior to any site visit, contacts were established with appropriate host personnel, appointments were made, holdings data requested, and the schedule set in place. Time limits as well as geographic location were considered in arranging the sequence of the site visits, since visits to several institutions and individuals were frequently scheduled in one day.

A successful on-site visit depended on how well plans were formulated during this stage of the preparation, and the rapport that could be established with host personnel. As site visits extended farther and farther from the home site, project staff relied more and more heavily on local staff to locate, arrange and inventory their holdings. They assisted further by providing additional contacts and leads, in some cases making the calls themselves.

Providing the local community members with some background on the project, explaining Penn State's role specifically, and outlining the upcoming itinerary in their county promoted a sense of camaraderie.

Before any on-site visit, an exhaustive list of all known newspaper titles for a given county was prepared from county histories and newspaper bibliographies. This roughly constructed title list, detailing title proper, variant titles, place of publication, beginning and ending dates, frequency, and preceding and succeeding title changes, acted as a quick ready reference guide while in the field. It provided valuable data needed when constructing a title's history from a short run or even from a single issue.

INITIAL ON-SITE ACTIVITIES

Upon arrival at a site, the team met host personnel, toured the facility, located all collections (e.g., microfilm, original copy, current issues, archives, special collections, stacks, etc.) to familiarize themselves with the arrangement of the collections. Since collections at an institution can be in several places or even different buildings, access to these areas was ensured prior to the time of the site visit.

Curators of museums and historical societies often expected to conduct tours of their facility for team members, so it was prudent to build in extra time for this when possible.

Once apprised of the local situation, the team obtained the appropriate signature on the Public Accessibility Agreement (which grants permission to make public a site's holdings). Information on interlibrary loan policies was collected, or the Name-Address Directory record was updated. Other preliminary activities included checking for locally prepared indexes to newspapers, and gathering information on the existence and location of microfilm master negatives. Once the preliminary courtesies and activities were complete, the actual work began.

CATALOGING, RELATED PROBLEMS AND POSSIBLE SOLUTIONS

The problems and corresponding solutions which follow are broadly grouped into sections dealing with identifying titles, linking titles, updating cataloging and gathering holdings data.

Identifying Newspaper Titles

Discrepancies in bibliographical sources and county histories created problems in terms of establishing title history (beginning and ending dates), linking title changes, and identifying the title proper from loosely used masthead titles, running titles and variant titles. This could only be clarified by actually examining the newspapers themselves. Community historians frequently provided local histories which shed further light on title changes. When conflicting historical data was introduced, best judgment prevailed.

Due to imposed time restraints, when examining a lengthy run of a particular title, a thorough examination of every volume or reel of microfilm was impractical, so the possibility of overlooking a title change in the middle of a run does exist. To reduce the risk of error, much title research was done prior to each visit, and the prepared title list previously described was consulted frequently throughout. Additionally, reels of microfilm were selected at random, and the first few frames (targets) on the reel were examined; bound volumes of paper copy were also selected and spot-checked to pinpoint title changes. In adhering to new cataloging rules (treating each title change as a new title), project catalogers made new discoveries as they identified previously unrecorded titles within a lengthy run.

The team also found that some institutions, following earlier cataloging rules, file newspapers (and all previous title changes) under the *latest* title. Prior knowledge of preceding title changes facilitated location of these changes within the run. Where no history existed, the entire run of a title was examined even more closely.

Many times the team worked in an isolated environment which lacked bibliographical/reference tools and resource people. This created a problem when ethnic newspapers were found, if they appeared in a language unfamiliar to either team member. If a copier was available, the masthead and publisher's statement was copied. If not, it would be transcribed by hand as authentically as possible, and resolved later by foreign language experts and/or reference tools.

Linking Newspaper Titles

One of the most challenging and frustrating aspects of on-site cataloging was the inability to see the whole history of a title and its links when cataloging from one or two single issues. Often a fifty-year history had to be constructed from scant data. Again the preconstructed title list provided critical information on some of the variant titles and links, and served as a base from which to begin the lengthy and time-consuming process of linking.

After a site visit, once the collected data was assimilated, return visits or calls were often needed to clarify cataloging information, especially for volume and issue numbers of ending dates between title changes. These missing links of a newspaper title did not come to light until all data had been collected from all sites. By maintaining cordial relations with contact personnel, project staff could often acquire missing information by follow-up phone calls. A return visit was planned if missing data was extensive.

Updating Cataloging

While at a major university library, the team cataloged a newspaper called the *Tioga Banner*, from the earliest issue held, dated April 11, 1848. Later on at the local public library, they discovered a *Tioga Banner* dated November 26, 1846. This situation often occurred and it was necessary to update the previous cataloging. The frequency with which this occurred could be partially controlled by carefully examining holdings information received from various sites and determining in advance who had what. But, however well-planned, surprises nevertheless happened.

A different but related problem occurred when the team encountered titles published in counties other than the one being canvassed at the moment. There was no way to determine whether the issue in hand was earlier than one previously cataloged since all previously completed workforms were not accessible on every visit. In such cases, it was necessary to catalog these titles, resulting in some duplication of effort; more information was better than not enough. The team decided that it was quicker to catalog these items again than to maintain and consult a list which would include all titles cataloged and the earliest date on which cataloging was based.

Another aspect of the same problem surfaced in the following situations: even after all newspaper titles for a given county had been cataloged, and the records input on OCLC, new information (e.g., earlier issues found, ending dates discovered, local data records added) was often found which required constant and ongoing OCLC updating. If a title was suspect, the cataloging workform was held until further information could be gathered. On other occasions, updating cataloging was done as necessary.

Gathering Holdings Data (Local Data Records—LDR's)

Determining an institution's newspaper holdings was based on verification of any previously received holdings lists plus an examination of its actual files. On occasion, a complete inventory had to be done before work could begin. Many problems hampered the gathering of this information, some of which are detailed below.

Microfilm-related problems (local data record—FM copy). Microfilm-related problems can be categorized in two ways.

The first category relates to the arrangement of microfilmed newspaper titles (or the *lack* of arrangement) at an institution.

In some cases, the microfilm was in no particular order, so time was taken to organize the collection. Sometimes microfilm was filed by the *latest* title, making it difficult to locate earlier title changes. Knowing in advance some of the preceding titles and dates was helpful. In some instances, newspapers were filed by *collections*, not individual titles (e.g., Harrisburg Newspaper Collection). The institution's guides were then used to locate titles, even though this constituted an additional step.

When more than one title was filmed on a reel, the reel could only be filed in one place, posing difficulties in locating the other titles. In still other cases, microfilm of newspapers was interfiled with microfilm of periodicals, census data, etc., and had to be isolated to be examined.

The second category of microfilm problems relates to the individual reels of microfilm.

It is an understatement to say that microfilm boxes are notorious for being mislabeled. Experience had taught us to assume nothing and to check everything. Even targets were checked to verify microproducers, since information on the box often differed from information on the film. Some specific problems encountered were: several titles were sometimes filmed together on one reel; single titles were filmed backwards or were not in chronological order; miscellaneous and scattered issues of a single title sometimes appeared on one reel; retakes and duplicate issues were filmed at the end of a reel; poor filming, and filming from torn and faded issues made for poor legibility. In one instance, the title used on the target differed from the actual title filmed. If this particular reel had only been spot-checked, the true title would have been overlooked.

Equipment (microfilm readers). At some institutions, where only one microfilm reader was available, it was necessary to have the reader reserved during the site visit.

Another problem with microfilm readers was that many were antiquated, and hence difficult to operate, required manual rewinding, or were defective. A broad knowledge of how to operate a variety of microfilm readers and a good sense of humor were mandatory.

Original copy problems (local data record—OR copy). Similar problems occurred when examining paper copy. In a long newspaper run, bound volumes lacked arrangement, or were interfiled with other bound volumes. Frequently they were stacked 20 volumes deep on a 15-foot-high shelf, earliest date on the bottom. Spines were often incorrect, and frequently several different titles were bound together. Others were bound backwards. Where such problems existed, more time was required to collect or verify holdings data. To obtain data on current subscriptions, the team consulted host personnel, since current issues were usually housed in a different location.

While these problems may exist in most institutions and are not unique to on-site cataloging, they were magnified by the fact that there was a limited amount of time available to the team to resolve these problems on-site.

WORKING CONDITIONS

Working conditions from site to site varied greatly. While not considered problems, per se, some of the more unusual conditions encountered are described below. It was necessary to be prepared to work in less-than-ideal circumstances.

Perhaps the most challenging experience to date was spent in a "vault" (a very tiny room), with dim lighting, no ventilation, no work space except for a podium and small desk, no chairs, and no facilities nearby. The vault had been unopened for 30 years, and a thick layer of dust had accumulated. In the vault were 155 separate titles which had to be cataloged in the one day scheduled for that visit.

At another site it was necessary to climb a ladder to gain access to the garage attic where papers were stored. The team also worked in a crawlspace in a newspaper publisher's office, in several unlit attics and in poorly lit, damp, unfinished basements.

Experience has shown that at most sites team members will locate more newspapers than were reported on the institution's inventory. These unexpected finds were frequently located by checking again in person with host personnel, or by carefully looking around the site for "forgotten" issues.

CONCLUSIONS

The problems encountered by the Penn State staff engaged in on-site cataloging are only one aspect of the complex process of planning and executing a site visit. Phases which were not discussed include the details of pre-site planning and the lengthy cataloging and follow-up activities which occur after the site visit has been completed.

Planning carefully for the visit was the best insurance for a successful and positive experience. Time was built in whenever possible for the tours and ceremonials required at many sites. When advised to bring a flashlight and wear coveralls, the team concurred. Warnings and other signals given during phone contact by newspaper owners, e.g., "the papers are somewhat difficult to access" and "plan on being here for a while since they're not in order," were taken to heart.

It must be emphasized, however, that the excitement of discovering new and unrecorded titles to enhance the OCLC database, meeting authors, collectors and historians in the field, and working in a variety of surprising situations far outweigh the difficulties associated with on-site cataloging.

Perspectives on the Pennsylvania Newspaper Project at the University of Pittsburgh

Faye Leibowitz
Cathy Sorensen

ABSTRACT. The bibliographic phase of the Pennsylvania Newspaper Project (PaNP) is described in terms of organization and procedures. During the first year of the PaNP, cataloging at five sites distributed geographically throughout Pennsylvania was implemented. Overall project direction is provided at the State Library of Pennsylvania and CONSER authentication for Pennsylvania newspaper cataloging is performed at the University of Pittsburgh (Pitt). The article emphasizes activities at the University of Pittsburgh and documents procedures and recommendations by the staff at Pitt. Unique complexities of cataloging newspapers and recording holdings information are examined. An innovative system of profiling has been developed to allow for the inclusion, into OCLC, of the holdings of small repositories and private individuals.

INTRODUCTION

The Pennsylvania Newspaper Project (PaNP) is part of the United States Newspaper Project (USNP), which is funded by the National Endowment for the Humanities (NEH). The State Library of Pennsylvania is the contractor agency within Pennsylvania. It provides statewide coordination and is responsible for the overall administration of the project. The Pennsylvania Newspaper Project is divided into three phases as is normal in all U.S. Newspaper Program statewide projects. Pennsylvania's Phase I planning grant was funded from July 1, 1983–June 30, 1984. Phase II (bibliographic control, the current PaNP phase) began in January 1985 and involves the cataloging, inventorying

---

Faye Leibowitz, MLS, and Cathy Sorensen, MLS, are Pennsylvania Newspaper Project catalogers at the University of Pittsburgh Libraries, University of Pittsburgh, Pittsburgh PA 15260.

The authors wish to thank the many archivists, historians and library staff members who have shared their time and expertise. In particular, we thank the Technical Services and Special Collections staff at the University of Pittsburgh, Bob Harriman and Todd Butler at the Library of Congress, and Rian Miller-McIrvine of PALINET for their patience, encouragement, and help. A special thank you to the National Endowment for the Humanities, for having had the insight to preserve America's past and its legacy to the future.

and condition evaluation of newspapers. Phase III (preservation) will provide for microfilming of selected titles. All completed cataloging, holdings and preservation workforms are stored at the State Library, to be used during the preservation phase of the project. It is anticipated that there will be some overlays between Phase II and Phase III within Pennsylvania.

This article describes the organization and workflow of the Pennsylvania Newspaper Project with emphasis on the work at the University of Pittsburgh site.

CATALOGING SITES

The Pennsylvania Newspaper Project was designed to have six cataloging centers geographically distributed around the state. Four cataloging sites were activated for the initial year, beginning January 1, 1985. The four are: the State Library of Pennsylvania, the Historical Society of Pennsylvania, Pennsylvania State University, and the University of Pittsburgh. Each of the cataloging sites outside of the State Library is a sub-contractor. The Free Library of Philadelphia had received separate funding, under Title I of the Library Services and Construction Act, to catalog its newspapers. The Free Library agreed to follow all project standards and has been actively involved with the official PaNP participants throughout 1985.

The cataloger at the State Library of Pennsylvania, at the time of the writing of this article, is cataloging the library's extensive newspaper collection. After the State Library's collection has been completely cataloged the cataloger will visit sites within a 16 county area of Harrisburg.

The Historical Society of Pennsylvania holds the greatest number of individual newspaper titles in the State. The cataloger at the Historical Society is concentrating on cataloging this library's collection. After work at the Historical Society has been completed, the cataloger will catalog titles held at repositories within a five county radius of Philadelphia.

The Pennsylvania State University (PSU) is responsible for cataloging newspapers published and held within a 15 county area of north central Pennsylvania, and for collecting holdings data for papers published elsewhere but held in repositories in the area. PSU catalogers complete cataloging, local data record and preservation worksheets and forward them to Pitt, where they are revised, authenticated, and input into OCLC.

The University of Pittsburgh Library System (Pitt), a full CONSER member, is responsible for the verification and approval of entries into the CONSER data base. As a result, cataloging records from the other three Pennsylvania newspaper cataloging sites are currently revised and authenticated by Pitt newspaper catalogers. In addition, the University of Pittsburgh is responsible for cataloging all Pennsylvania titles held at Pitt, as well as those held at repositories located within a 10 county area in southwestern Pennsylvania. Pitt catalogers are also responsible for updating Pitt's union list of serials.

Cataloging sites for titles held in 11 northwestern and 10 northeastern Pennsylvania counties will be designated in the future.

The Assistant Director for Technical Services for the University of Pittsburgh Library System serves as the Project Director, for the Pitt Newspaper Project site. The PaNP personnel at Pitt includes two full-time professional librarians and one part-time student assistant. The librarians are responsible for cataloging, recording holdings, and compiling preservation information, in addition to authenticating work from other sites. The Pitt serials cataloging staff provides technical support, and one of the serials catalogers also serves on the PaNP Technical Committee. The student assistant's primary responsibility is inputting cataloging and local data records into OCLC, although the student also performs many other tasks.

TRAINING

Training began in January 1985 for the Newspaper Project catalogers and their student assistant at the University of Pittsburgh. Prior to formal training sessions at OCLC and at the State Library of Pennsylvania, one of the University of Pittsburgh catalogers began to survey and do preliminary cataloging of newspapers. This preliminary work was done to familiarize the cataloger with specific problems encountered in newspaper cataloging, as well as to gain experience in compiling holdings and preservation summaries.

Formal training sessions for catalogers were held at OCLC and at the State Library of Pennsylvania. Two representatives from the PaNP attended the three day intensive training session at OCLC, which included instruction in union listing, and searching and creating entries for the name-address directory, as well as cataloging. This training session was conducted by OCLC and LC staff. In addition, the Assistant Director of the Office of Preservation for the National Endowment for the Humanities outlined preservation goals.

The two Pennsylvania catalogers who attended the OCLC training session subsequently conducted the cataloging training portion of a workshop for all Pennsylvania Newspaper Project participants held at the

State Library in early February. Participants were also trained in Local Data Record (LDR) creation by PALINET staff, and in preservation by staff from the Pennsylvania Historical and Museum Commission, Division of Archives and Manuscripts. The preservation training included instruction in identifying various types of microfilm (i.e., diazo, silver positive, negative, etc.)

IDENTIFYING PROCEDURES

Developing procedures for newspaper project activities is a complicated matter. (For background information on USNP procedures, see Harriman's article in this volume.[1]) The first step is to identify project goals. These were generally outlined at the OCLC training session, and consist primarily of:

1. Locate libraries or other repositories with holdings of newspapers.
2. Identify the libraries' holdings, and record them in standard newspaper local data records format.
3. Catalog the newspapers according to the rules outlined in the *Newspaper Cataloging Manual*,[2] *AACR2*, and LC rule interpretations.
4. Describe the physical format and condition of the newspapers.
5. Identify the repository's interlibrary loan policies (ILL), and enter them into the OCLC Name-Address Directory (NAD).

The means for accomplishing these activities depends largely on the size of the collection being cataloged, the extent of the holdings of a particular newspaper at the library, and whether cataloging records for the newspaper are already on OCLC.

LOCATING HOLDINGS

Although historically, newspapers have lacked extensive bibliographic control so often afforded other library materials,[3] most of Pitt's newspaper holdings have been documented, either in OCLC local data records, or in a local serials union list. In addition Pitt's holdings are often represented in the major bibliographic reference sources and union lists.[4]

Catalogers at the University of Pittsburgh have concentrated on collecting information about Pennsylvania newspaper titles, although a large number of out-of-state titles are also held by local libraries. This concentration is necessary so that all major newspaper repositories in Western Pennsylvania can be surveyed within the 3–4 year period proposed for the completion of the bibliographic phase of the project. If time allows, holdings of out-of-state papers will also be recorded near the end of the project. It is believed that other states' holdings of their own titles will be more complete than Pennsylvania's holdings; therefore, it will be more efficient for them to catalog their own titles. However, if Pitt catalogers locate a first issue (vol. 1, no. 1) of an unique out-of-state title, the item will be cataloged.

Emphasis is placed on collecting more complete holdings for rare titles. Standard bibliographic reference sources aid in determining titles for which holdings have not yet been located, or those which are located in only one or two repositories. Absence of a title in standard union lists helps to identify it as a rare title.

The Pitt newspaper catalogers originally intended to catalog newspapers in alphabetical order as listed in *Pennsylvania Newspapers: A bibliography and union list*, 2d ed. by Glenora E. Rossell. It soon became apparent that it is much more time efficient to catalog newspapers in chronological bibliographic order, i.e., catalog the earliest title, then its succeeding titles. It is better to concentrate on a unilateral succession of newspaper titles first, such as "weeklies," before progressing to the related dailies and semi-weeklies. Otherwise, the task may seem unmanageable if the library holds complete runs of related dailies, weeklies, semiweeklies, etc., dating back 150 years. Such was the case of the Pittsburgh Post-Gazette, which eventually comprised over 40 related titles. Tree diagrams are especially helpful in reconstructing a newspaper run, particularly when various editions are published simultaneously, or for complex runs with many variations including merges, splits, absorptions, and related editions (Figure 1).

Locating newspapers on microfilm is quite a challenge. Microfilm copy of related titles (e.g., daily and weekly editions) and unrelated titles are often filmed together in sets under a generic title, such as "Harrisburg Newspapers." This set actually represents nearly 50 titles on 53 reels of microfilm. Titles are often boxed and shelved under latest or earliest entry. The majority of title changes of the Pittsburgh Post-Gazette are boxed and shelved as Pittsburgh Post-Gazette. Actual changes in the title are not noted on the microfilm boxes. Splicing film to separate titles would be costly and time consuming. Cross referencing of these title changes is accomplished by means of "dummy" boxes which can easily be misshelved.

Often, newspapers on microfilm are listed on local serial records only by the title that is on the box in which they are stored. Titles are occasionally located for which no listing exists in the Pitt union list, and sometimes, not all libraries with holdings of a particular title are listed as having holdings. Therefore, it is helpful to develop a procedure of

44   THE UNITED STATES NEWSPAPER PROGRAM: CATALOGING ASPECTS

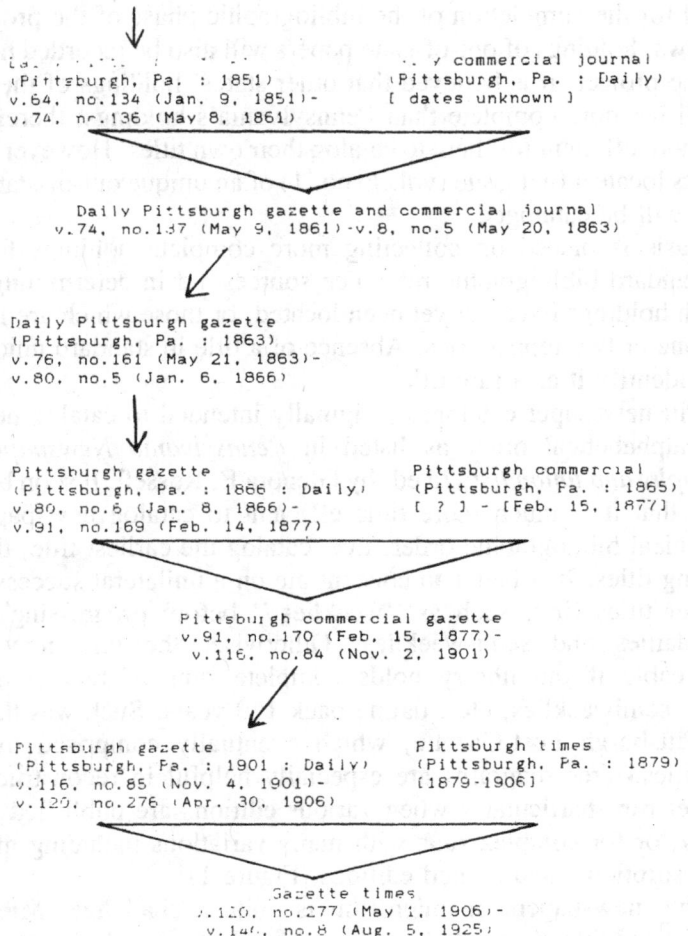

FIGURE 1. Partial tree diagram. Arrows indicate "continues," triangles indicate "merge." Begin with the earliest known or available title, such as a daily, and work on its succeeding titles. Once it is brought up to date or up to its latest title, begin adding related editions. Save preceding and succeeding merges, splits, related titles, etc., as a separate set of records to catalog after the initial run is completed.

searching all locations which might have the newspaper. For example, recent issues of a current newspaper may be in the current newspaper stacks, in addition to being held in microfilm. Current issues of a Black newspaper might be shelved in the Afro-American Library, rather than in the current newspaper stacks.

Locating hard copy titles to be cataloged is also complex. Newspapers bound in volumes are often heavy and cumbersome, and in varying stages of disintegration. The volumes must be handled with care. However, the sense of reliving history more than compensates for size, weight and the two hundred years worth of accumulated dust. It is not unusual to find boxes and bound volumes labeled "miscellaneous newspapers." These may contain single issues of dozens of related or unrelated titles. Often newspapers are bound chronologically, combining dozens of unrelated titles which were published during a particular year. Other volumes are bound "geographically," combining many titles from a single state or city. One title may be held in five or six different locations.

Newspaper holdings at the Pitt campus are housed in seven locations. Six of these locations are within Hillman Library, the main library building. The seventh is located on the sixth floor of the Cathedral of Learning, two minutes walking distance from Hillman Library. Catalogers have found it helpful to introduce themselves to the staff at each collection, and on occasion arrange for a special orientation to the collection. In addition to the staff who are specifically involved in the technical services area, considerable assistance has been received from the archivists, librarians and paraprofessionals who work in the special collections and microfilm departments.

SEARCHING

Once holdings have been located it is necessary to search OCLC. In some instances, it is better to search OCLC before looking at the actual newspapers. In other cases it is better to catalog first and search later, editing any existing record if necessary. If you are reasonably sure that the library has a complete run of a newspaper, the authors believe it is better to search OCLC first for all related titles, and print off the screens. Editing can be done directly on the OCLC printouts of the bibliographic records. If you expect to find single issues or short runs of newspapers, it may be more effective to catalog first and search later. This problem may be resolved if a portable personal computer is available, which can be carried to various locations and used to dial up and search OCLC for titles as they are found. The Pitt project staff expects to test the use of portable microcomputers in the field during the project's second year.

Searching newspaper titles on OCLC has become more complicated following the system enhancements of April 1985, in which publisher, rather than place of publication, is displayed.[5] Thorough searching of OCLC is necessary to avoid creating duplicate records. This is especially true with regard to "generic" titles such as Daily News, or Times. It is necessary to search the title proper, as well as variant titles. Searching by uniform title rather than title proper usually results in a successful search. However, title searches must also be done to retrieve so-called "dumped"[6] records which have no uniform titles, and should be upgraded or reported for deletion if found. Qualifying title searches by /ser and a range of years will limit the number of records retrieved. Care must be taken, however, to also qualify searches by "????", in order to retrieve records containing "u's" or blanks in the date area of the fixed field.

Three possibilities may occur when searching a title on OCLC:

1. The title searched is not in the database (no record is retrieved.)
2. Only one record is retrieved for the title searched.
3. Multiple records are retrieved, including those linked to the title searched, variant titles, etc.

The third possibility occurs frequently, especially when searching the shorter, more generic titles.

CATALOGING HINTS

After OCLC searching has been completed and appropriate reference sources have been searched, cataloging can begin. (Figures 2 and 3). It is important to note unusual characteristics which aid in identifying relationships between titles. Scan the newspaper before and after a masthead change. Editorials often inform the reader of absorption, splits, mergers, suspensions, etc. Note differences in running titles, publisher or content. Anniversary issues can provide useful hints for reconstructing the history of a newspaper. However, these special issues cannot be used as a basis for bibliographic description in many cases. They often lack characteristics usually attributed to newspapers, such as a masthead, and are often published in magazine format.

Mottos lending a political or ethnic slant should be noted. Standard terms representing ethnic or political 'intended audiences' should be entered in the subfield i of the call number (CLNO) field on the LDR. The development and use of intended audience terms is described by Danky[7] in an article in this volume. Official organs of an ethnic or political organization or other corporate body should be included in the bibliographic record. To determine whether the appropriate corporate heading has been established, check the OCLC and local Name Authority Files. This access point could prove very important for researchers.

Changes in volume/numbering may signal other changes in the publication. A new title may continue its numbering from a previous title, or in the case of a merge, it may adopt both numbering systems. An article by Griffin and Cole, dealing with numbering peculiarities[8] has been particularly helpful in dealing with newspaper numbering peculiar-

PENNSYLVANIA NEWSPAPER Cataloging Record	OCLC # 12020223	LCCN 010 sn85-54563
Sources Searched	Entries Searched	

FIXED FIELD

TYPE 16 a	BIB LVL 17 s	Gov Pub 28	LANG 35-37 eng	SOURCE 39 d	S/L ENT 34 0
REPR 22	ENC LVL 117 7	Conf pub 29	CTRY 15-17 pau	Ser tp 21 n	Alphabt 33
Indx 31 u	Mod rec 38	Phys med 22 e	Cont 24-27	FREQUN 18 c	PUB ST 6 d
DESC 118 a	Cum ind 32 u	Titl pag 30 u	ISDS 20	REGULR 19 r	DATES 7-14 1894—1896

Physical Description
007 h ǂb ǂc ǂd ǂe ǂf ǂg ǂh ǂi ǂj

VARIABLE FIELDS

Languages	Authentication	LC Call Number
041 __ b	042 msc	050 __ b

Uniform Title Heading
130 0 0 Pittsburgh post (Pittsburgh, Pa. : 1894 : Semiweekly)

Title and Statement of Responsibility
245 0 4 The Pittsburgh post.

Variant Titles
246 1 3 Semi-weekly post

Edition
250 Semi-weekly ed.

Imprint
260 0 0 Pittsburgh, Pa. : ǂb Post Printing & Publishing Co., ǂc 1894-

Physical Description
300 v.

Current Frequency
310 Semi-weekly

Former Frequency
321

Numeric/Alphabetic/Chronological Designation
362 0b Jan. 2, 1894-

Series
362 10 Ceased with Apr. 4, 1986 issue?
4 __ __ __ __

PDE-1610 (1/85)

FIGURE 2. Cataloging workform, side 1.

ities. A change in frequency from daily to semiweekly to monthly may signal the cessation of a newspaper. When possible, note in the subfield b of the 310 and 321 fields the dates of frequency changes. Noting variations in frequency clarifies the record. Often, dates of frequency changes on bibliographic records are the only indication that a newspaper has changed frequency over time, rather than having been published in

```
Notes

    580      Also published in daily edition called: Pittsburgh post (Pittsburgh, Pa. :
             1887 : Daily).


Added Entries




Geographic Access for Newspapers
752  United States ǂb Pennsylvania   ǂc Allegheny        ǂd Pittsburgh.

Linking Entries

    775 1    ǂt Pittsburgh post (Pittsburgh, Pa. : 1887 : Daily) ǂw(OCoLC)2266182

    780 00   ǂt Semi-weekly post ǂw(DLC)sn 85054561



Holdings  Library _____    OCLC Code _____
    ☐ Hard Copy (Newsprint)



    ☐ Microfilm




Comments (Temp Info)                              | Originator          | Reviewer/Reviser
                                                  | (Initials & Date)   | (Initials & Date)
```

FIGURE 3. Cataloging workform, side 2.

several editions. A perpetual calendar can be a useful cataloging tool. It can be helpful in establishing frequency (by determining days of the week that a newspaper is published.)

Often publishers statements or subscription statements give leads to editions or other frequencies. In such cases, a note stating "also issued in" other edition/s is created. If the actual title of the other edition is known, a 775 field should be added.

Note gaps which suddenly occur in an otherwise fairly complete run. They may actually be suspensions, possibly due to natural disasters, such as the fire which suspended publication of the Progressive American (sn85-54663), or an invasion during the Civil War which curtailed publication of the Franklin Repository (sn85-54674) for a short period. Scanning issues on either side of the actual change can sometimes provide insight into the reason for suspension.

If a title being cataloged is linked to other records these would be discovered while thoroughly searching OCLC. These links must be attached to the title being cataloged as well as to the related titles in the data base unless they are determined to be incorrect. If they are found to be incorrect they must be deleted from all related records. It is especially important to evaluate links which have been cited from reference sources.

All information recorded should be gathered from the actual newspaper being described. Note any external information supplied by citing the source. This verifies that the information supplied was not contained in the actual newspaper. This aids catalogers at other sites in substantiating or changing our cataloging based on concrete evidence obtained from additional issues of the newspaper.

PITT CONSER PROCEDURES

In addition to responsibility for cataloging southwestern Pennsylvania newspapers, Pitt is also responsible, as a CONSER library, for authenticating cataloging done at other sites in Pennsylvania. Cataloging workforms (but not surrogates) are usually received from each site once or twice a month. At the time of writing of this article, the procedures followed by Pitt staff are:

1. Check to make sure that all mandatory fields and sub-fields required in the document *"United States Newspaper Program Base Level Cataloging"* are present.
2. Search OCLC to determine that the record is not a duplicate of another record in the database.
3. Check all linking fields for consistency.
4. Contact catalogers at the appropriate sites should questions arise.
5. Determine that the bibliographic description is consistent with rules outlined in the *Newspaper Cataloging Manual*, *USNP Bibliographic Notes*, *AACR2*, and *LC Rule Interpretations*.
6. Compare holdings as represented on the LDRs with the bibliographic record to assure that dates are consistent.

7. Call the Library of Congress for assistance in resolving extremely complex cataloging problems, if necessary.
8. Attach 010 and 042 fields to the record.

HOLDINGS

After bibliographic records have been updated, local data records with holdings data are attached. Newspaper LDRs (Figure 4) differ from other serial LDRs in several respects. Newspaper LDRs are used to differentiate between various formats held for a particular title in lieu of creating separate bibliographic records for each format. See Graham's article in this volume: "*Rethinking National Policy for Cataloging Microform*

```
                        LDR Worksheet

   TITLE:      Pittsburgh post (Pittsburgh, Pa. : 1894 : Semiweekly)

   LC#:        sn 85-54563

   OCLC#:      12020223

   Hld lib:    PIT2                   Copy:         FM

   CLNO: ǂb Pittsburgh post, reels 91-92    ǂi _____

   SCHD:  ǂe   5
          ǂn   Scattered issues wanting.


          ǂy   s=(1893:11:1-1895:12:31)(1896:4:3)

   SIHD:  ǂe   5
          ǂy   1894-1895, 1896


   Does the Library have a locally maintained index for this title? [ ] Yes [X] No
       If yes, indicate scope:
```

FIGURE 4. LDR workform.

Reproductions".[9] Codes in the "COPY" area of the LDR fixed field identify the format for which holdings are recorded.[10] The codes are:

OR —Original
FM —Microfilm
FMM —Microfilm master
FC —Microfiche
FCM —Microfiche master
OP —Microopaque
OPM —Microopaque master
FX —Facsimile, Eye-readable reprint

Prior to August 15, 1985, separate LDRs were not created for microform masters. Instead, microform masters were identified by a code in the subfield n of the summary copy holdings display (SCHD) field of a microform LDR. However, because masters could not be located by indexing the SCHD field, the Library of Congress revised the practice, and now separate LDRs for microform masters are created.

The LDR holding library (Hld Lib) field reflects the unique structure of the Pennsylvania Newspaper Project OCLC profile. Existing OCLC three character codes are used when describing holdings of OCLC member repositories. However, PaNP catalogers collect holdings from many small repositories and private individuals' homes, which have never been assigned OCLC codes. For information on site visits see the Kellerman and Wilson article in this volume.[11]

OCLC developed a system, in conjunction with the State Library and PALINET, whereby a three letter code was assigned for each county within Pennsylvania. A fourth letter code, representing an individual repository, is attached to the county code. For example AWF represents Columbia county; the letter C represents Berwick Historical Society, therefore the Berwick Historical Society is coded AWFC. The letters "B"-"J" in the fourth character position will be assigned to larger repositories which are open to the public. The letter "A" is always a default character, representing smaller repositories or private individuals. If a holding library is coded AWFA, this indicates that the holdings are located either at a small Columbia County repository or held by a private individual residing in Columbia County. Since most of the cooperating smaller repositories or individuals do not have formalized ILL policies they will not require separate entries in the OCLC Name-Address Directory. Instead the State Library of Pennsylvania will maintain a confidential list of names and addresses and will serve as an intermediary between patrons and holding sites. This system protects their anonymity while making their unique holdings accessible.

The "CLNO" (call number) field of newspaper LDRs is being used in rather innovative ways. An important aspect of the University of Pittsburgh project is to insure that local data records reflect exact location. The subfield b of the CLNO field has been adapted to reflect local shelving information (e.g., "Harrisburg newspapers, reel 12" or "Pittsburgh post-gazette, reels 46–52"). The subfield i of the CLNO field is used to identify ethnic, political or other terms which will constitute valuable research tools. See James Danky's article.[12]

The SCHD field begins with subfield n (optional) which may contain a standard phrase pertaining to the completeness or quality of issues held (e.g., "scattered issues," "some issues mutilated," or "issues lacking.") When recording microform holdings the subfield y begins with a code (or codes) which identify the microform type (i.e., s = positive microfilm service copy, sm = microfilm negative service copy, etc.). This code is followed by an equals sign and the holdings recorded within angle brackets.

Newspaper LDRs describe holdings in terms of specific dates held (year:month:day) rather than describing holdings in terms of "volume" and "number." This type of notation is preferable because researchers generally ask for a particular date or range of dates of a newspaper rather than a particular volume number.

Subfield y contains, in angle brackets, detailed dates held. For example, issues for the following dates: May 3 and 14, 1853; June 6, 1854; Jan. 6, 1856–Mar. 8, 1856; Nov. 12, 1858–Dec. 6, 1862, would be written in this style:

SCHD $y <1853:5:3,14><1854:6:6><1856:1:6-3:8><1858:11:12-1862:12:6>

Angle brackets are used in the SCHD field to identify beginning and ending dates of holdings and to denote gaps in a run. Titles currently received begin with an angle bracket and end with a hyphen only. Commas denote gaps between months or days held.

The SIHD (Summary Institution Holdings Display) field contains no brackets, and utilizes commas and/or hyphens to identify the range of years held. The examples cited above would be written in this manner:

SIHD $y 1853, 1854, 1856, 1858-1862

Prior to August 1985 all microform information in the SCHD field was enclosed in square brackets. This field included a code representing the microform producer(s). However, it was decided that square brackets and the microproducer codes were of limited value, and should not be included.[13]

RELATIONSHIP TO PITT INTERNAL RECORDS

The University of Pittsburgh maintains a serials union list in two formats: (1) a locally maintained tape updated in batch and (2) online with OCLC. The lists include holdings of all titles held by all Pitt campuses. One of the unique responsibilities of the Pitt cataloging site is the updating of the serials union list records to accurately reflect the holdings of each title, including the addition of appropriate links to previous or succeeding titles.

The process of updating Pitt's internal union list is extremely time consuming at the present time, because Pitt's locally maintained union list is not online, and all information must be checked in either the hard copy or microfiche union list of serials. Forms must be filled out for all changes or additions to the holdings information. This situation is expected to be eliminated in the near future as the Pitt union list of serials is completely online with OCLC as well as maintained in a local batch system. It is planned to load the Pitt union list into the University's NOTIS system in 1986. Shortly thereafter, the local batch union list will be discontinued. Pitt's LDRs for newspapers in the OCLC online union list were initially entered in the standard serials LDR format. Newspaper Project catalogers routinely upgrade these LDRs to reflect current newspaper LDR format.

PRESERVATION

In addition to cataloging and recording holdings of newspapers, the Pitt newspaper catalogers are responsible for describing their physical condition. This will aid in achieving the ultimate goal of preserving newspapers through microfilming. PaNP participants use a standard workform (Figure 5), which is attached to the cataloging and local data record workforms, to record preservation information. These "condition reports" will be stored at the State Library of Pennsylvania until the preservation phase of the project. Information about physical condition of newspapers is recorded at the time the item is cataloged. Information about multiple copies of issues is also recorded on the workform, as is information relating to microfilm condition and type.

Surprisingly enough, the more recent newspapers often face the most immediate danger of disintegration.[14] The high fiber content of the earlier newspapers (those published before approximately 1870) make them considerably more durable, and thus they are not in immediate physical jeopardy. The cheaper newsprint of the last one hundred years has not stood the test of time nearly as well as the paper produced prior to the advent of modern technology.

PENNSYLVANIA NEWSPAPER Condition Report PDE-1610 (2/85)	Recorded by		Date
Title Pittsburgh post (Pittsburgh, Pa. : 1894 : Semiweekly)			OCLC # 12020223
☐ HARD COPY (NEWSPRINT)			
Bindings	☐ Open flat	☐ Open flat with pressure	☐ Tight, broken, or powdery
Paper	☐ Flexible	☐ "Dry" but turns	☐ Brittle (breaks on turning)
General coloration	☐ Bright	☐ Marginal discoloration (dirt, stain)	☐ Uniformly darkened
TREATMENT/HOUSING			
Notes			

☐ MICROPRINT

[XX] MICROFILM

☐ Negative or [XX] Positive

[XX] Silver ☐ Diazo ☐ Vesicular

☐ 16 mm [XX] 35 mm ☐ 105 mm

Reduction ratio: ☐ 24x ☐ 42x ☐ 96x [XX] other unknown

Eye readable: [XX] Yes ☐ No

Clear: [XX] Yes ☐ No

Master: Made by Microfilm Corp. of Pa.

Exists ☐ Yes ☐ No unknown

Missing Issues: ☐ Yes ☐ No

COMMENTS

FIGURE 5. Preservation workform.

STATISTICS

Statistics keeping for work done at Pitt is somewhat complex because Pitt is responsible for processing different types of information for each Pennsylvania site. For example, the Pitt staff are responsible for actual input of all information from cataloging and local data record workforms for the site at Pennsylvania State University, but are responsible only for authenticating records which the Historical Society of Pennsylvania and State Library of Pennsylvania input into OCLC.

Generally, Pitt staff have been recording all statistics on the standard USNP Monthly Statistics forms distributed by the Library of Congress. An additional heading is added for "records used but not enhanced." This identifies records which Pitt staff have not edited, but to which they added holdings. Another heading is added to identify how many name authorities were established. Separate statistics are kept for each site, noting the number of newly authenticated records, and any LDRs added for each site. The Pitt staff lists "LDRs created" by OCLC symbol, to justify any storage charges assessed to that library's symbol. For example, all LDRs created for any University of Pittsburgh (PIT) library are listed under PIT. Because Penn State collects holdings from many different sites, each site's OCLC symbol is listed separately (e.g., UPM = Penn State, PCB = Central Pennsylvania District Library Center, AWFC = Berwick Historical Society, etc.).

FUTURE CHANGES

The staff at Pitt is investigating the possibility of obtaining additional help without cost to the project. One possibility is to offer a practicum for a graduate student in Library Science. The student would aid the catalogers in a variety of tasks, including evaluation of physical condition of newspapers, locating and recording holdings, assisting in updating local Pitt serials union list information, and cataloging of several titles. The student would receive academic credit for working on the project, but would not receive a salary.

Many changes are anticipated for technical services at the University of Pittsburgh in the next five years. Naturally, these changes will have an impact on the Newspaper Project. Pitt newspaper catalogers are making extensive use of personal computers for word processing and are examining other capabilities, such as storage and retrieval of information for statistical and other purposes. A name, address, and title index to small repositories' and private individuals' holdings is being maintained on personal computers.

The installation within the coming years of the NOTIS automated library system will undoubtedly affect Newspaper Project procedures, and open new possibilities. It may be feasible to experiment with NOTIS' file creation capabilities and Boolean searching as they apply to newspaper records.

In addition, the Pitt newspaper catalogers hope to utilize electronic mail in the near future to communicate with newspaper catalogers at other sites in Pennsylvania. Due to the nature of the work, which requires newspaper project staff to be away from their work stations most of the time and therefore unavailable for the necessary long-distance phone calls, electronic mail is a priority.

CONCLUSION

Cooperation and open lines of communication are the backbone of a successful Newspaper Project. Several meetings have been held for Pennsylvania Newspaper Catalogers. These meetings are valuable for maintaining consistency in cataloging, as well as for strengthening the Newspaper Project "Network."

The "Network" ultimately transcends state boundaries. Input from catalogers at other State and Repository Projects is helping the Pitt staff to improve its work while at the same time experiences at Pitt will benefit others. Cooperation at the national level will continue to be vital to the growth and development of the United States Newspaper Project.

NOTES

1. Robert Harriman, "Coordination of Cataloging Practices in the United States Newspaper Program," *Cataloging and Classification Quarterly* 6(4): (Summer 1986).
2. Robert Harriman, *Newspaper Cataloging Manual* (Washington: Library of Congress, 1984).
3. Jean Whiffin, "Union Catalogues of Serials: Guidelines for Creation and Maintenance with Recommended Standards for Bibliographic and Holdings Control—Chapter 9.1 Newspapers," *Serials Librarian* 8(1): 71–75 (Fall 1983).
4. Major references which have been particularly helpful are: Clarence Brigham's *History and Bibliography of American Newspapers 1690–1820*; Winifred Gregory's *American Newspapers 1821–1936*; Library of Congress' *Newspapers in Microform, 1983*; Pennsylvania Historical Commission's *A Checklist of Pennsylvania Newspapers*; Glenora Rossell's *Pennsylvania Newspapers: A Bibliography and Union List*, 2d ed.; *Union List of Serials*; IMS . . . *Ayer Directory of Publications*.
5. OCLC, *"Technical Bulletin,"* No. 154: 3.
6. In July of 1976, OCLC loaded a tape containing the serials union list of the University of Pittsburgh. A number of records for newspapers were included in the load. The bibliographic information was normally incomplete. Now the USNP cataloging sites have the opportunity to upgrade the old tape loaded newspaper records AACR2 and CONSER standards. Or, the records should be reported as duplicates if appropriate (as in the case of finding an authenticated record).
7. James Danky, "Newspapers and Their Readers: The United States Newspaper Program's List of Intended Audience Terms," *Cataloging and Classification Quarterly* 6(4): (Summer 1986).
8. David E. Griffin and Jim E. Cole, "Note Worth Noting: Notes Used In AACR2 Serials Cataloging," *Serials Review* 10(3): 52–55 (Fall 1983).
9. Crystal Graham, "Rethinking National Policy for Cataloging Microform Reproductions," *Cataloging and Classification Quarterly* 6(4): (Summer 1986).
10. *United States Newspaper Program Input of Holdings into OCLC*: 2.

11. Rebecca A. Wilson and Lydia Suzanne Kellerman, "Challenges of On-Site Cataloging," *Cataloging and Classification Quarterly*, 6(4): (Summer 1986).

12. Danky, *op. cit.*, p. .

13. Robert Harriman, "*United States Bibliographic Notes*, No. 5," Library of Congress (Aug. 15, 1985).

14. Library of Congress Preservation Office, "*Newsprint and Its Preservation.*" Preservation Leaflet No. 5 (Nov. 1981).

The Newspaper Cataloging Manual and AACR2

Jim E. Cole

ABSTRACT. The rules for description in Harriman's *Newspaper Cataloging Manual* are compared to those found in Chapter 1 (General Rules for Description) and Chapter 12 (Serials) of AACR2, and the pertinent Library of Congress rule interpretations that have appeared in *Cataloging Service Bulletin*. Some of the differences among the documents, both major and minor, are discussed.

Paragraph 0.1 of the General Introduction to the second edition of the *Anglo-American Cataloguing Rules* (AACR2)[1] states that the rules "are not specifically intended for specialist and archival libraries, but it is recommended that such libraries use the rules as the basis of their cataloguing and augment their provisions as necessary." This statement has been taken quite literally. Since the publication of the new code in 1978, the library community has witnessed the appearance of an ever-growing number of sets of rules and manuals covering special types of materials and published with varying degrees of authority. This paper, it is hoped, will serve as an introduction to one of these manuals—Robert Harriman's *Newspaper Cataloging Manual*,[2] written for use by the United States Newspaper Program and published by the Library of Congress in 1984. It will attempt to compare the rules for the bibliographic description as found in the manual to those in Chapter 1 (General Rules for Description) and Chapter 12 (Serials) of AACR2, and the pertinent Library of Congress rule interpretations (LCRIs) in *Cataloging Service Bulletin* (CSB). It will examine the bibliographic description area by area and point out some of the differences, both major and minor, found among the various documents.

Harriman states in paragraph 0.4 (n)[3] of the manual that the rules contained therein follow the numbering pattern of AACR2, Chapter 12, and that he has attempted to incorporate pertinent provisions of Chapter 1 of the code, as they would be applied to newspapers, as well as relevant

---

Jim E. Cole is Assistant Professor and Serials Cataloger, 204 Farks Library, Iowa State University, Ames, IA 50011. Cole is serving as a cataloging supervisor for the Iowa Newspaper Project and was the American Library Association, Resources and Technical Services Division, Serials Section liaison to the Committee on Cataloging: Description and Access, from 1983 to 1985.

© 1986 by The Haworth Press, Inc. All rights reserved.

information from Library of Congress rule interpretations. He adds, though, that he is not implying that "this manual should be used without reference to or consultation of AACR 2. Rather, it should be viewed as a working tool designed to be a guide to the most common cases of newspaper description. It is expected that catalogers will continue to see AACR 2 as their primary source of documentation." Thus the cataloger should apply the provisions of the manual for the common cases and refer to AACR2 itself for the less frequently encountered situations. Difficulties may be said to exist for the cataloger, however, because the numbering system of Chapter 12 of AACR2 is not followed exactly (some rules are of necessity renumbered in the manual), and because at times phrases or entire sentences of the rules found in AACR2 have been omitted from the corresponding rules in the manual. In general, the differences among the three documents may be classified as follows:

1. Rules in the manual and AACR2 contain conflicting provisions. (Here the provisions in the manual clearly take precedence.)
2. Rules found in AACR2 are completely omitted from the manual. (Here, since the manual contains no conflicting provisions, one must apply AACR2 itself if the situation covered therein arises.)
3. Rules in the manual, while closely following AACR2 wording, nevertheless omit phrases or sentences found in AACR2. (Are these omissions deliberate and to be considered conflicts between the manual and AACR2, or are they manifestations of the common case/rare case problem, with AACR2 then prevailing? The cataloger must decide.)
4. Rules in the manual fail to incorporate recent Library of Congress rule interpretations or contain provisions conflicting with them; further information regarding the applicability of the LCRIs is not provided by *USNP Bibliographic Notes*, issued irregularly by the Library of Congress in the form of memoranda. (In her introduction to the manual, Henriette Avram says that "it is assumed that further refinement of rules and procedures will evolve. The manual will be updated, as necessary, to reflect these changes." Thus the approach may be correctly taken here that the provisions of the LCRIs have been purposely disregarded, since the manual has not been updated to reflect them, nor are they mentioned in the *Notes*.)

GENERAL RULES

Since modern newspapers have neither title pages nor covers, the chief source of information is of necessity the caption. Without explicitly defining the terms, the manual substitutes the term *masthead* for AACR2 *caption*, in turn calling the AACR2 *masthead* the *publisher's statement*. Because the publisher is oftentimes not named in the masthead, the manual changed the list of prescribed sources of information for the Publication, Distribution, Etc., Area by including the publisher's statement and omitting the colophon, which newspapers generally lack.

The manual is intended solely for use in preparing MARC records for entry into the CONSER database. Since the space-dash-space separating areas of the description is machine-generated, rule 12.0C(n) does not direct the cataloger to precede the first element of most areas by a period-space-dash-space. Rules for the punctuation of individual areas other than the first merely say to "precede this area by a full stop." Rule 12.0C(n) also says that one space is to follow a period, while LCRI 1.0C (CSB 24) at times requires two spaces. The rule is silent about the use of brackets within a given area or adjacent areas. In these cases one must refer to AACR2 1.0C.

Until winter 1985 when it amended LCRI 1.0E (covering the language and script of the description), the Library of Congress said that if items published after 1820 showed peculiar forms of letters (e.g., "v" for "u," "i" for "j"), one should regularize these forms according to modern usage. However, in CSB 27, this statement was revised. Among other changes, the 1820 date was changed to 1800, with special rules for pre-1801 publications. The manual has not reflected these changes, still retaining the 1820/1821 reference point in 12.0F(n), which interestingly covers inaccuracies rather than language and script.

TITLE AND STATEMENT OF RESPONSIBILITY AREA

AACR2 rule 1.1B1 appears in abridged form in 12.1B1(n) of the manual. Because of this, rule 12.1B5(n) directs the cataloger to include an alternative title as part of the title proper, but the manual does not say how it should be punctuated. This must either be inferred from the example (in AACR2 examples are illustrative but not prescriptive), or the cataloger must consult AACR2 1.1.B1. Somewhat related to this is the fact that LCRI 21.30J (CSB 27) says that when cataloging a work whose title proper includes an alternative title, the cataloger should include an added entry for the first part of the title (the part preceding the "or" or its equivalent) if it consists of three or less words that are filed on; 12.1B5(n) merely specifies an added entry for the alternative title.

May one abridge a long title proper of a newspaper? The manual is silent on this, perhaps because it should not be done, perhaps because newspaper titles are rarely if ever to be considered too long, and when necessary, one would follow AACR2 1.1B4. One clearly must consult AACR2 1.1B5 when transcribing words appearing only once that are intended to be read more than once; AACR2 1.1B8 for the selection of the title proper if the title appears in more than one language or script on the chief source of information (admittedly not a rare situation, since 12.1D(n) covers the transcription of parallel titles); and AACR2 12.1B6 about the treatment of dates or numbers in the title proper that vary from issue to issue. In this latter case, rule 12.1B2(n) may be applied to some extent, but the rule doesn't describe the proper use of the ellipsis in this situation.

The newspaper program employs the innovative "master record" concept. A newspaper is described as it was originally published, with other physical forms—reprints, microfilm, etc.—indicated in the local data records giving the participants' holdings. (See paragraph 0.7(n) in the manual.) Thus, no general material designation is given.

While 12.1D(n) says that for items published in the United States one should record all parallel titles appearing on the chief source of information, it lacks any provision for the order in which they should be recorded; one must apply AACR2 1.1D1. Although rule 12.1A1(n) says to precede the title of a supplement or section by a period, one must follow the provisions of AACR2 12.1B3-12.1B5 for recording the section or supplement title, since the manual contains no rules for recording them.

EDITION AREA

Because of the "master record" concept, one may not include a reprint or reissue statement (AACR2 12.2B1 type e) in the edition area. Special interest edition statements (AACR2 12.2B1 type b) are also omitted from the list given in 12.2B2(n), while it adds frequency edition statements (12.2B2(n) type d). The example given under type d is of interest: L'Osservatore romano.—[Weekly ed.]. The edition statement is in English, the title in Italian. Perhaps edition statements supplied from sources other than the masthead are always to be in English, because rule 12.2B1(n) says uniform phrases should be employed whenever possible. According to AACR2 1.0E, this would at times not be the case, since the rule says to "give interpolations into these areas in the language and script of the other data in the area." Also, when should an edition statement be supplied by the cataloger? The manual says it may be supplied from "other sources," perhaps including reference sources. It would seem wise to apply LCRI 1.2B4 (CSB 13), even though it deals with revisions, and to supply an edition statement only if the catalog records needed would show exactly the same information in the areas beginning with the Title and Statement of Responsibility Area and ending with the Physical Description Area.

Rule 12.2B4(n) says that if an edition statement appears in two or more languages or scripts, one should give the statement that is in the language or script of the title proper, and also the parallel statements, each preceded by an equals sign. This is similar to the optional provision added to AACR2 1.2B5 (CSB 25) for recording parallel edition statements; the Library of Congress announced in CSB 25 a tentative decision not to apply the option.

The manual's contents section for the Edition Area lists rules 12.2C(n), Statement of responsibility relating to the edition, 12.2D(n), Subsequent edition statement, and 12.2E(n), Statements of responsibility relating to a subsequent edition statement. It is aesthetically disturbing that rules specifically mentioned in the contents are not actually printed in the manual. One again must consult AACR2 (rules 1.2C-1.2E) when necessary.

NUMERIC AND/OR OTHER CHRONOLOGICAL, OR OTHER DESIGNATION AREA

The manual adheres extremely closely to the AACR2 wording found in Area 3. Differences exist, however, between the printed text and the LCRIs for the corresponding AACR2 rules. Rule 12 3E(n) says when a serial has more than one separate system of designation, to record the systems in the order in which they are presented in the chief source of information. LCRI 12.3E (CSB 23) broadens this somewhat, saying that the alternative numbering systems need only be presented in the source used in recording the first system (the numbering may be found in the publisher's statement, for example, with only the date of issuance in the masthead). The same LCRI also says to prefer to record as the first a system that uses the form of a volume number and internal number, e.g., v. 7, no. 2. This may or may not be the first numbering system given on the chief source of information, but brings a needed standardization, since it is not always possible to determine the order of the numbering systems as presented on the source.

The manual lacks the discussion regarding "one serial or two" caused by the repetition of numbering systems (LCRI 12.3G, CSB 26). LCRIs 12.3B1 and 12.3C1 (CSB 23) have also not been incorporated into the manual.

PUBLICATION, DISTRIBUTION, ETC., AREA

Rule 12,4B8 (n) in the manual is taken from AACR2 1.4B8, which says to describe the publication in terms of the first named place of publication, distribution, etc , and the corresponding publisher, etc. It further directs the cataloger to add the place and name of subsequent entities in certain circumstances. However, the deletion of rule 1.4B8 and its replacement by a revision of 1.4D5 were announced in CSB 25. The revised 1.4D5 directs the cataloger to describe the publication in terms of the first named publisher, distributor, etc., and the corresponding place.

Rule 12.4C3(n) says to add the name of the country, state, province, etc., to the name of the place if necessary for identification or if necessary to distinguish the place from others of the same name. Unlike the corresponding rule 1.4C3, it does not say that the addition is to be in English, following the forms prescribed by rule 23.2A. Rule 12.4C6(n) requires the cataloger to follow a supplied place name with a question mark whenever it isn't named in the item; rule 1.4C6 of AACR2 says to do this only if the place is uncertain.

Rule 12.4D3(n) contains what appears to be an incorrect example—": Printed by Edes & Gill,". This seems incorrect for two reasons. First, Edes & Gill seem to be a manufacturer and not a publisher, distributor, or the like, and are thus not covered by the rule (see 12.4D7(n)). AACR2 rule 1.4G2, saying that when recording the place and name of the manufacturer, one should follow the instructions found in 1.4B-1.4D, is omitted from the manual. Second, if Edes & Gill are, as indicated, the manufacturer, the example would lead one to believe that the phrase "Printed by" should not be omitted when the name of a manufacturer is recorded.

The manual contains no rule similar to AACR2 1.4F6, which provides for recording the copyright date or date of printing in the absence of a date of publication. Here it must be assumed that AACR2, although not directly contradicted, may not be applied. Rule 1.4F7 of AACR2 says that if no date of publication, copyright date, or printing date can be assigned from the item, one should give an approximate date. Rule 12.4F5(n), on the other hand, says that if no *publication* date is given in the first issue, one is to give an approximate date. Here the manual parallels the rule for recording a place of publication, etc., not given in the item: even if the cataloger is certain, the date must be recorded as at best approximate. This rule in the manual contains an additional sentence not found in AACR2: "This should occur only in the very rarest cases in newspaper cataloging." This sentence has completely changed the basic concept in AACR2 and the LCRIs, where a date given as chronological coverage or date of issuance in Area 3 is not considered an imprint date. Few newspapers bear actual dates of publication; the date of publication must in general be extracted from the chronological designation and is still recorded without brackets.

PHYSICAL DESCRIPTION AREA

Rule 12.5C1(n) of the manual says to describe an illustrated paper as "ill." unless the illustrations are principally commercial in nature, when they may be optionally qualified with "(chiefly advertisements)." The manual does not provide for the use of the extreme list of types of illustrations found in AACR2 rule 2.5C2, to which Chapter 12 directs the cataloger.

AACR2 rule 2.5D3 (to which the cataloger is also directed by Chapter 12) says that if the height of the publication varies by more than two centimeters, one is to give the smallest and largest sizes, separated by a hyphen. Rule 12.5D2(n) says that the difference must be more than four centimeters.

SERIES AREA

Since newspapers are only extremely rarely if ever issued originally in a series, this area is omitted from the newspaper cataloging record, which uses the "master record" concept.

NOTE AREA

While AACR2 1.7A3 says the source of a quotation taken from the item must be given if it is other than the chief source of information, rule 12.7A3(n) of the manual does not require this. Similarly, it does not mention the use of prescribed punctuation in notes referring to certain areas of the description.

The manual provides for an order of notes entirely different from AACR2. The order AACR2 prescribes is as follows:

> frequency; languages; source of title proper; variations in title; parallel titles and other title information; statements of responsibility; relationships with other serials; numbering and chronological designation; publication, distribution, etc.; physical description; accompanying material; series; audience; other formats available; indexes; contents; numbers; copy being described and library's holdings; "with" notes; and, item described.

The manual's order, clearly affected by the order of notes prescribed by CONSER, is the following:

> frequency; extent of publication; item described; source of title

proper; variations in title; general notes; publication, distribution, etc.; physical description; accompanying material; numbering and chronological designation; audience; supplements; other formats available; languages; statements of responsibility (except editors); indexes; editors; and, relationships with other serials.

A certain liberty has been taken with the "500" MARC notes, however, in that they are greatly rearranged from the AACR2 order. For instance, the note on the item described is last in AACR2 and for most serials can be the last note tagged 500. In the manual's order, it is the first note tagged 500.

How does one define a title fluctuation? Under AACR2 LCRI 21.2A (CSB 25), duration does not appear to be a factor in the decision; instead, the publisher's intent and the random spacing of a few issues with the variant title are important. However, because of the high frequency of newspaper title changes and the short duration of many of them, and also influenced by the pragmatic desire to limit the number of records needed to catalog the complete run of a newspaper, Harriman has stated that duration of the variant title is a primary consideration in newspaper cataloging. In *USNP Bibliographic Notes*, no. 3, he states

> If a newspaper title fluctuates back and forth over a period of time, and the variant title appears continuously for no more than a year at a time, separate records are not justified. Choose the title of the first issue (or earliest issue in hand) as the title proper. Record the variant title as an access point and in a note . . . If, however, a newspaper is published under the variant title for more than one year at a time, separate records for each title are required.[4]

Thus with newspapers one finds frequent notes dealing with what to the general serials cataloger would be a title change requiring a separate record.

Frequently newspapers are related to others which either have not been located or which are not known to exist. In such situations, 12.7B18(n)k directs the cataloger to add "(non-extant)" after the titles of these papers in the note area.

CONCLUSION

Harriman's *Newspaper Cataloging Manual*, issued under the authority of the Library of Congress, has brought standardization to an aspect of serials where general standardization on the national level was before lacking. The manual may well be considered this century's single most significant contribution to the total bibliographic control of newspapers.

It is hoped that this paper has established two important points: (1) One may not correctly catalog newspapers according to the prevailing national standard without consulting pertinent rules in AACR2 itself. As Harriman clearly states in paragraph 0.4(n), AACR2 remains the cataloger's primary source of documentation, (2) one may not correctly catalog newspapers according to the prevailing national standard by using AACR2 alone. The manual contains important and, at times, substantial, variations from AACR2, generally caused by the material being cataloged.

The relationship between the manual and any LCRIs not incorporated into the manual is rather ambiguous. A seemingly correct, albeit conservative, approach is to disregard these LCRIs until the manual is revised to include them, or an announcement is made in *USNP Bibliographic Notes* regarding their applicability. Two documents could clarify this and a similar problem about the relationship of the manual to AACR2: a table, updated quarterly, showing which AACR2 LCRIs the cataloger should follow (including those already incorporated into the text of the manual), and which the cataloger should ignore; and a table showing which rules of AACR2, either not printed in the manual or abridged therein, the cataloger should consult when necessary.

NOTES

1. *Anglo-American Cataloguing Rules*. 2nd ed. Chicago: American Library Association, 1978.
2. Harriman, Robert. *Newspaper Cataloging Manual*. CONSER/USNP ed. Washington, D.C.: Serial Record Division, Library of Congress, 1984.
3. The various rules from the *Newspaper Cataloging Manual* are distinguished from those of AACR2 by a parenthetical *n*, e.g., 0.1(n), 12.0(n).
4. "21.2A2(n). Variations in Title," *USNP Bibliographic Notes* 3 (1984):3.

Rethinking National Policy for Cataloging Microform Reproductions

Crystal Graham

ABSTRACT. Current national cataloging policy requires the creation of unique cataloging records for an original publication and each of its microfilm reproductions. Such redundant entries are difficult to decipher and expensive to produce and maintain. The case of serial publications is most urgent, especially due to the proliferation of preservation microfilming efforts and union list projects. The master record concept used in the United States Newspaper Project offers a viable alternative method. Librarians should lobby to have the single record approach adopted as national policy.

Current cataloging policy mandates the creation of a separate cataloging record for a microform reproduction of a previously published work. While the original publication and each of its reproductions present the very same intellectual work, a unique cataloging record must be generated for each one. At a time when shrinking library budgets are forcing cut-backs in acquisitions and essential library services, this wasteful practice demands reconsideration. The expense of creating and storing such "duplicate" records is not justifiable in terms of patron service; in fact, the redundancy complicates the search process.

The national policy for cataloging microform reproductions is actually a Library of Congress rule interpretation, adopted as a makeshift solution to the problem of applying Chapter 11 of AACR2 to this type of material. The published text of AACR2 prescribes a totally new record for each manifestation of a title, with the bibliographic description based on the physical piece in hand. This policy met with widespread opposition from librarians who contend that such a policy obfuscates identification of the original text.[1] The flavor of this position is captured in the following excerpt from an eloquent essay by Louis Charles Willard:

[The requirement of Chapter 11 of a totally new record for each

---

Crystal Graham, Serials Cataloger, New York University, New York, NY 10012.

The author gratefully acknowledges the ideas of the panelists at the ALA RTSD Serials Section Research Libraries Discussion Group meeting held January 6, 1985: Linda Bartley, Marjorie Bloss, Thomas Bourke, Nancy Romero, and, especially, Jeffrey Heynen. Special thanks to Suzanne Hanen for her editorial assistance.

microform reproduction] results from an obsession with principle to the exclusion of common sense. It fails to recognize that the most important thing about a microform reproduction is not that it is a microform but that it is a *reproduction*. To the library making the acquisition, the scholar seeking the title, and indeed, the cataloger describing the work in hand, the specific form of the copy, reproduction, or (in the case on non-microforms) facsimile, is subordinate, that is to say, accidental, to its primary reality, which is that it is an imitation, textually an exact imitation.[2]

Under pressure from librarians to devise an alternative to the requirement to base the bibliographic description on the reproduction rather than on the original publication, the Library of Congress issued a rule interpretation to Chapter 11.[3] This interpretation also specifies the creation of a separate bibliographic record for a microform reproduction of a previously published work, but the bibliographic description is based on the originally published item, with some additions: a general material designation [microform] added to the title proper (245 $h) and a note describing the reproduction added to the body of the description (533 field). The appropriate chapters of AACR2 are applied when describing the original publication (e.g., Chapter 2 for printed books; chapter 12 for serials), as are the AACR2 rules for choice and form of access points. Additional content designators used in the MARC records include an 007 field (for recording preservation information) and fixed field codes (008) relating to the reproduction. This rule interpretation and concomitant MARC tagging policies have been adopted by all major American bibliographic utilities as network standards.

The Library of Congress rule interpretation is undoubtedly an improvement over the rules as originally published. Yet changing the basis of the bibliographic description from the reproduction to the original does not resolve the problems of wastefulness and confusion posed by multiple records for a single entity.

The current policy is untenable for all types of materials, but most extreme when applied to serial publications, hence this article. Libraries frequently own both paper copy and one or more microform reproduction of a given serial title. Current issues of a periodical may be received in paper copy, while the backfile is retained in microform. A gap in the paper copy run may be filled with issues on microfilm. Multiple reproductions may also be held. For example, some institutions are switching from microfilm to microfiche for all serial subscriptions available in that more compact format. As librarians become more preservation-conscious, libraries are filming serial runs locally, and coordination of these efforts is resulting in the exchange of partial runs filmed by various agencies. When multiple records from many libraries holding different versions are brought together in a serials union list, the duplication is even more confusing, for patron and librarian alike.

THE PROBLEM FOR PATRONS

Current standards for cataloging microform reproductions do not facilitate user access. Multiple records for the same title are confusing, whether they represent different physical manifestations or different micropublishers in the same format. The records for *New leader (New York, N.Y.)* in Figures 1 and 2 illustrate the similarity of the cataloging records for the original print version and the microform reproduction. While a general material designation and reproduction note are present on the record for the microfilm, it is fairly difficult to ferret the information out of the bibliographic record. A user is more likely to discern the fact that the library owns the microfilm from the call number designation.

In COM and online catalogs, the notes portion of the bibliographic record is often suppressed in displays. Without that information, the records for different manifestations may appear to be duplicate records. The example of the *Federal register* in Figure 3 illustrates the brief record display which appears to contain three such "duplicates." Examination of the full records in Figures 4–6 shows that the first is for microfiche, the second for the National Archives microfilm, and the third for the UMI microfilm.

Even more alarming than the potential for confusion created by these "duplicate" records is the possibility that multiple records for the same title may be overlooked by patrons. Once users have located a record for the item desired, they often stop searching. When the specific issue sought is not held in the format represented by the first record located, the user may conclude that the issue is not available in the collection. As Thomas Bourke, Head of Microforms at the Research Libraries of New York Public Library, put it succinctly: "The smaller the number of records, the greater the user's chances of finding the right one."[4]

"Duplicate" records are likely to be overlooked when they file together. When the records have been created under different catalog codes, causing the entries to differ, there is even more confusion. Looking again at the *Federal register* example, Figure 7 shows an additional record in the catalog for the paper copy of the title. The cataloging for this record was formulated under a previous cataloging code and bears little resemblance to the AACR2 microform records found in the online catalog (Figure 3).

FIGURE 1

```
Tam.         New leader (New York, N.Y.)
                The New leader --
                Vol. 1, no. 1 (Jan. 19, 1924)-
                -- New York, N.Y. : [New Leader
                Publishing Assoc., 1924-
                   v. :  ill. ;  28-57 cm.

                Weekly, 1924-Aug. 28, 1961;
                Biweekly, Sept. 18, 1961-1966;
                Biweekly (except July and Aug.), 1967-
                Title from masthead.
                Numbering irregular.
                Newspaper format, 1924-1943.
                Magazine format, 1944-
                An official publication of the
                Socialist Party, May 15, 1926-May 23,
                1936; official organ of the Social
                                   (Cont'd on next card)
 B SL            841221           841221  NNU
 C000305         CG /DJM           A1     84-S814
```

```
Tam.         New leader (New York, N.Y.)  The New
                leader... New York, N.Y. : [New
                Leader Publishing Assoc., 1924-
                                        (CARD  2)
                Democratic Federation, May 30, 1936-
                June 29, 1946.
                Issues for 1924-July 4, 1955
                published by the New Leader Publishing
                Assoc. (also called New Leader
                Assoc.); issues for July 11, 1955-
                published by the American Labor
                Conference on International Affairs.
                Masthead of issue for Dec. 24, 1927:
                New leader and American appeal.
                Caption of issues for Oct. 13, 1928-
                Aug. 28, 1937 includes phrase: "with
                which is combined the American appeal,
                                   (Cont'd on next card)
 B SL            841221           841221  NNU
 C000306         CG /DJM           A1     84-S814
```

```
Tam.         New leader (New York, N.Y.)  The New
                leader... New York, N.Y. : [New
                Leader Publishing Assoc., 1924-
                                        (CARD  3)
                founded by Eugene V. Debs."
                Indexed by:
                   Reader's guide to periodical
                literature ISSN 0034-0464
                   Public Affairs Information Service
                bulletin ISSN 0033-3409
                Continues: New York leader.
                Absorbed: American appeal (Chicago,
                Ill.), Dec. 3, 1927.
                Absorbed in part by: Russian
                affairs, 1945.
                ISSN 0028-6044

                                   (Cont'd on next card)
 B SL            841221           841221  NNU
 C000307         CG /DJM           A1     84-S814
```

FIGURE 1 (continued)

```
Tam.         New leader (New York, N.Y.)  The New
             leader...  New York, N.Y. : [New
             Leader Publishing Assoc., 1924-
                                           (CARD   4)

                1. Socialism--Periodicals.  2. Labor
             and laboring classes--Periodicals.   3.
             World politics--Periodicals.  4. Civil
             rights--Periodicals.  I. Socialist
             Party (U.S.)  II. Social Democratic
             Federation of America.  III. American
             Labor Conference on International
             Affairs.  IV. Title: New leader and
             American appeal.  V. Title: New leader
             with which is combined the American
             appeal.
B SL            841221              841221 NNU
C000308         CG /DJM        A1          84-S814
```

THE PROBLEM FOR CATALOGERS

Bibliographic network standards pose a dilemma for catalogers with regard to microform cataloging. The networks require a member library to derive its cataloging record from another member's record for the publication when such a record is already present in the database, regardless of the rules under which the record was formulated. If no record is present for the specific manifestation to be cataloged, the member library is required to formulate a new record according to AACR2. This causes many problems.

Searching for a record representing the particular manifestation in hand can prove time-consuming. The cataloger must decide when it is appropriate to adapt existing copy and when an original record should be created. For example, if several different micropublishers have issued microfilm reproductions of the same title, should a new record be input for each reproduction? If the same micropublisher issues a publication in both microfilm and microfiche, must one search for separate records?

The requirement for a new record to be in accordance with AACR2 in terms of description and access points complicates the process of cataloging different versions of the same publication. The rules for cataloging serials changed drastically from AACR1 to AACR2. First and foremost, the AACR1 description was based on the most recent issue, while under AACR2 the description is based on the earliest issue. The choice of entry is often different, especially since AACR1 prescribed issuing body as the main entry far more frequently than does AACR2. The forms of access points are also frequently different under the two

FIGURE 2

```
Tam.         New leader (New York, N.Y.)
Film            The New leader [microform] --
R1           Vol. 1, no. 1 (Jan. 19, 1924)-
-            -- New York, N.Y. : [New Leader
R16,         Publishing Assoc., 1924-
R274            v. :  ill. ;  28-57 cm.

                Weekly, 1924-Aug. 28, 1961;
             Biweekly, Sept. 18, 1961-1966;
             Biweekly (except July and Aug.), 1967-
                Title from masthead.
                Numbering irregular.
                Newspaper format, 1924-1943.
             Magazine format, 1944-
                An official publication of the
             Socialist Party, May 15, 1926-May 23,
             1936; official organ of the Social
                              (Cont'd on next card)
B SL              841221        841221 NNU
C000400           CG /DJM       A1     84-S815


Tam.         New leader (New York, N.Y.)  The New
Film            leader [microform]...  New York,
R1           N.Y. : [New Leader Publishing
-            Assoc., 1924-
R16,                                      (CARD  2)
R274         Democratic Federation, May 30, 1936-
             June 29, 1946.
                Issues for 1924-July 4, 1955
             published by the New Leader Publishing
             Assoc. (also called New Leader
             Assoc.); issues for July 11, 1955-
             published by the American Labor
             Conference on International Affairs.
                Masthead of issue for Dec. 24, 1927:
             New leader and American appeal.
                Caption of issues for Oct. 13, 1928-
             Aug. 28, 1937 includes phrase: "with
                              (Cont'd on next card)
B SL              841221        841221 NNU
C000401           CG /DJM       A1     84-S815


Tam.         New leader (New York, N.Y.)  The New
Film            leader [microform]...  New York,
R1           N.Y. : [New Leader Publishing
-            Assoc., 1924-
R16,                                      (CARD  3)
R274         which is combined the American appeal,
             founded by Eugene V. Debs."
                Indexed by:
                   Reader's guide to periodical
             literature ISSN 0034-0464
                   Public Affairs Information Service
             bulletin ISSN 0033-3409
                Microfilm. [New York, N.Y.] : New
             York Public Library, 1955.  17 reels ;
             35 mm.
                Continues: New York leader.
                Absorbed: American appeal (Chicago,
                              (Cont'd on next card)
B SL              841221        841221 NNU
C000402           CG /DJM       A1     84-S815
```

FIGURE 2 (continued)

```
Tam.        New leader (New York, N.Y.)   The New
Film           leader [microform]...  New York,
R1             N.Y. :  [New Leader Publishing
-              Assoc., 1924-
R16,                                         (CARD  4)
R274        Ill.), Dec. 3, 1927.
               Absorbed: Russian affairs, 1945.
               ISSN 0028-6044



                                       (Cont'd on next card)
B SL              841221               841221 NNU
C000403           CG /DJM              A1      84-S815



Tam.        New leader (New York, N.Y.)   The New
Film           leader [microform]...  New York,
R1             N.Y. :  [New Leader Publishing
-              Assoc., 1924-
R16,                                         (CARD  5)
R274
               1. Socialism--Periodicals.  2. Labor
            and laboring classes--Periodicals.  3.
            World politics--Periodicals.  4. Civil
            rights--Periodicals.  I. American
            Labor Conference on International
            Affairs.  II. Socialist Party (U.S.)
            III. Social Democratic Federation of
            America.  IV. Title: New leader and
            American appeal.  V. Title: New leader
            with which is combined the American
            appeal.

B SL              841221               841221 NNU
C000404           CG /DJM              A1      84-S815
```

codes, especially for corporate bodies. Even the definition of what constitutes the title can vary, such as in the case of acronyms (which are rarely chosen as the title proper under AACR2).

Because the cataloging codes differ so much, the preparation of cataloging for microform reproductions is not merely a simple adjustment of existing cataloging copy. When records for the same entity differ in terms of choice and form of access points, the records do not file together as seen in the *Federal register* example above. This lack of collocation is often intolerable. To resolve the conflict, all existing records for all formats must be recataloged according to AACR2. When the existing record is latest entry, representing all former titles on one record, the situation is further complicated.

FIGURE 3

```
SER/PROD  Serials     PAR        NYUG85-S1092         Catalog         NYUG-CG
FIN ID NYUG85-S1092 - 1 record in SER - Record updated today
UPD
Federal register [microform]
   Vol. 1, no. 1 (Mar. 14, 1936)-
   -- [Washington, D.C. : Division of the Federal Register, the National
   Archives, 1936-
   v. ; 28 cm.

   ISSN 0097-6326
   LCCN: sf8419134
   ID: NYUG85-S1092              CC: 9110        DCF: a
- - - - - - - - - - - - - - - - - - - - - - - - - - - - - - - - - - - - - - -
   SHS NNU BREF7 MICRO 38 8509 Currently received. Limited retention. Retained
   until microfilm rec'd.

BREF7   \Micro\38\



SER/PROD  Serials     PAR        NYUG85-S1093         Catalog         NYUG-CG
FIN ID NYUG85-S1093 - 1 record in SER - Record updated today
UPD
Federal register [microform]
   Vol. 1, no. 1 (Mar. 14, 1936)-
   -- [Washington, D.C. : Division of the Federal Register, the National
   Archives, 1936-
   v. ; 28 cm.

   Series: National Archives microfilm publications.
   ISSN 0097-6326
   ID: NYUG85-S1093              CC: 9114        DCF: a
- - - - - - - - - - - - - - - - - - - - - - - - - - - - - - - - - - - - - - -
   SHS NNU BREF7 MICRO 36 8509 Not currently received. Permanently retained. 1-
   43 1936-1978

BREF7   \MICRO\36\



SER/PROD  Serials     PAR        NYUG85-S1094         Catalog         NYUG-CG
FIN ID NYUG85-S1094 - 1 record in SER - Record updated today
UPD
Federal register [microform]
   Vol. 1, no. 1 (Mar. 14, 1936)-
   -- [Washington, D.C. : Division of the Federal Register, the National
   Archives, 1936-
   v. ; 28 cm.

   ISSN 0097-6326
   ID: NYUG85-S1094              CC: 9114        DCF: a
- - - - - - - - - - - - - - - - - - - - - - - - - - - - - - - - - - - - - - -
   SHS NNU BREF7 MICRO 37 8509 Currently received. Permanently retained. 44-
   1979-

BREF7   \MICRO\37\
```

Not all microform cataloging records require expensive original cataloging or major recataloging. Sometimes consistent, good quality cataloging copy is available in the network database for each version of a publication. Yet it is still costly to search, produce, store, index, and file "duplicate" records. Staff time is wasted seeking interpretations of network standards and developing local policies. And the result of all this expenditure of effort and time is a labyrinth of confusing and redundant records.

The conventions for content designation of microform reproductions also cause confusion. The 533 field (the note describing the reproduction) and the 007 field (the content designators for preservation data) are both repeatable fields Logically one would assume that this repeatability was built into the MARC format so that various versions of microform reproduction could be represented on a single record. However the content designation standards state that, with the exception of dates, all the 008 fixed field data elements, which are not repeatable, must be coded for specific reproductions. Frequency of a microform reproduction is coded for the frequency of the microform (usually "unknown") rather than the frequency of the original. Its publication status is given as "current" whenever the filming agency has not reproduced the entire run, although the title itself may have ceased publication. The place of publication is coded for the location of the filming agency, not that of the original. Should our online systems ever include the capability to retrieve by place of publication, patrons looking for publications from, say, Lithuania, will turn away empty-handed, because we dutifully coded "nyu" as the place of publication of the microform reproduction.

Since the utility of current coding practices is questionable, these

FIGURE 4

```
SER/PROD   Serials      LON       NYUG85-S1092           Catalog          NYUG-CG
Record 1 of 1 - Record updated today
+
Federal register [microform]
   Vol. 1, no. 1 (Mar. 14, 1936)-
   -- [Washington, D.C. : Division of the Federal Register, the National
Archives, 1936-
   v. ; 28 cm.

   Daily (except Saturday, Sunday, and federal holidays)
   Title from cover.
   Issued Mar. 14, 1936-Mar. 23, 1951 by the Division of the Federal Register;
Mar. 24, 1951-Mar. 25, 1959 by the Federal Register Division; Mar 26, 1959-    by
the Office of the Federal Register.
   Indexed selectively by: Hospital literature index 0018-5736
   Indexed selectively by: Coal abstracts 0309-4979
   Indexed selectively by: Chemical abstracts 0009-2258
   Indexed selectively by: Energy information abstracts 0147-6521
   Indexed selectively by: Environment abstracts 0093-3287
   Microfiche. Washington, D.C. : Office of the Federal Register, 1982-
microfiches ; 11 x 16 cm.
   ISSN 0097-6326 0042-1219 = Federal register

SER/PROD   Serials      LON       NYUG85-S1092           Catalog          NYUG-CG
Record 1 of 1 - Record updated today
UPD
   1. Delegated legislation--United States--Periodicals. 2. Administrative law--
United States--Periodicals. I. United States. Office of the Federal Register.
II. United States. Federal Register Division. III. United States. Division of
the Federal Register.

   LCCN: sf8419134
   ID: NYUG85-S1092                    CC: 9110          DCF: a
```

FIGURE 5

```
SER/PROD  Serials     LON       NYUG85-S1093         Catalog         NYUG-CG
Record 1 of 1 - Record updated today
+
Federal register [microform]
  Vol. 1, no. 1 (Mar. 14, 1936)-
  -- [Washington, D.C. : Division of the Federal Register, the National
  Archives, 1936-
  v. ; 28 cm.

  Daily (except Saturday, Sunday, and federal holidays)
  Title from cover.
  Issued Mar. 14, 1936-Mar. 23, 1951 by the Division of the Federal Register;
  Mar. 24, 1951-Mar. 25, 1959 by the Federal Register Division; Mar 26, 1959-   by
  the Office of the Federal Register.
  Indexed selectively by: Hospital literature index 0018-5736
  Indexed selectively by: Coal abstracts 0309-4979
  Indexed selectively by: Chemical abstracts 0009-2258
  Indexed selectively by: Energy information abstracts 0147-6521
  Indexed selectively by: Environment abstracts 0093-3287
  Microfilm. Washington : National Archives, National Archives and Records
  Service, General Services Administration, 1950-     reels; 35 mm. (National
  Archives microfilm publications)
  Main series: National Archives microfilm publications
  ISSN 0097-6326  0042-1219 = Federal register


SER/PROD  Serials     LON       NYUG85-S1093         Catalog         NYUG-CG
Record 1 of 1 - Record updated today
UPD
    1. Delegated legislation--United States--Periodicals. 2. Administrative law--
  United States--Periodicals. I. United States. Office of the Federal Register.
  II. United States. Federal Register Division. III. United States. Division of
  the Federal Register. IV. Series: National Archives microfilm publications.

  ID: NYUG85-S1093            CC: 9114       DCF: a
```

conventions offer poor justification for the creation of separate records which could otherwise be described on a single record.

THE PROBLEM FOR UNION LISTS

When all the records for hard copy, microfilm, and microfiche are brought together in a union list, chaos ensues. Often there are multiple microform publications (e.g., UMI, Readex, Wisconsin Historical Society, plus locally preserved runs), so that the union list may contain half a dozen entries for the same serial title. Most union lists do not contain full bibliographic records. When the reproduction note is dropped in the union lists, all of the microform listings look identical (Look again at Figure 3).

According to AACR2, a uniform title is assigned to a serial to differentiate it from another serial with the same title. In some union lists, only the uniform title (130 field) is given, and the title proper (245) is not repeated. For example:

    Entry as: New leader (New York, N.Y.)
    not   New leader (New York, N.Y.). New leader.

Since the general material designation is given in the title field, and not in the uniform title,[6] a brief listing appears to contain duplicates:

New leader (New York, N.Y.)   Current issues only
New leader (New York, N.Y.)   1- 1924-

When additional holdings from other institutions are added, the listing becomes more and more confusing. If the various entries appear on different pages of a printed list, or on different sheets of a microfiche list, users often fail to find all of the entries. In the case of computer-generated lists, the machine filing can cause entries to be alphabetically separated, as in the following example:

Theatre
Theatre international
Theatre [microform]

While some display problems can be overcome by programming special manipulation of the general material designation, this increases the expense of producing the union list without addressing the fundamental problem.

OCLC, as the host system for a large number of online union lists,

FIGURE 6

```
SER/PROD  Serials    LON       NYUG85-S1094        Catalog         NYUG-CG
Record 1 of 1 - Record updated today
+
Federal register [microform]
   Vol. 1, no. 1 (Mar. 14, 1936)-
   -- [Washington, D.C. : Division of the Federal Register, the National
Archives, 1936-
   v. ; 28 cm.

   Daily (except Saturday, Sunday, and federal holidays)
   Title from cover.
   Issued Mar. 14, 1936-Mar. 23, 1951 by the Division of the Federal Register;
Mar. 24, 1951-Mar. 25, 1959 by the Federal Register Division; Mar. 26, 1959-
by the Office of the Federal Register.
   Indexed selectively by: Hospital literature index 0018-5736
   Indexed selectively by: Coal abstracts 0309-4979
   Indexed selectively by: Chemical abstracts 0009-2258
   Indexed selectively by: Energy information abstracts 0147-6521
   Indexed selectively by: Environment abstracts 0093-3287
   Microfilm. Ann Arbor, Mich. : University Microfilms International, [19--].
reels; 35 mm.
   ISSN 0097-6326 0042-1219 = Federal register

SER/PROD  Serials    LON       NYUG85-S1094        Catalog         NYUG-CG
Record 1 of 1 - Record updated today
UPD
   1. Delegated legislation--United States--Periodicals. 2. Administrative law--
United States--Periodicals. I. United States. Office of the Federal Register.
II. United States. Federal Register Division. III. United States. Division of
the Federal Register.

   ID: NYUG85-S1094           CC: 9114          DCF: a
```

FIGURE 7

```
SER/PROD   Serials      LON      NYUG1768512-S         Catalog            NYUG-CG
Record 24 of 75
+B
United States. National Archives and Records Service.
   Federal register.
   v. 1-    Mar. 14, 1936-
Washington [Office of the Federal Register, National Archives and Record
Service; distributed by the Supt. of Docs., U. S. Govt. Print. Off.]
   28 cm.

   Daily (except Saturday, Sunday, and official Federal holidays)
   Indexed by: Chemical abstracts 0009-2258
   Indexed by: Selected water resources abstracts 0037-136X
   Vol. 1-15, no. 39 issued by the National Archives.
   Indexes: Includes indexes.
   Supt. of Docs. no.: GS 4.107:
   ISSN 0097-6326 0042-1219 = Federal register

   I. United States. National Archives. II. Title.

   LCCN: 3626246
   035: (MnMULS)0759947
   ID: NYUG1768512-S              CC: 9665          DCF:
```

permits each union list group to decide how to represent holdings of microform reproductions. OCLC requires users to base bibliographic descriptions on AACR2, which specifies separate bibliographic records for each format of a title. For union list holdings statements, OCLC recommends attaching the holdings statements for reproductions to the bibliographic records that describe each one, and then making references to records for different formats. (See example of this method in Figure 8). However OCLC recognizes strong arguments for using a single record in a union list. Therefore, while realizing that "this procedure contradicts current Anglo-American cataloging rules," OCLC permits users to use the hardcopy record for all manifestations of the same title.[7] (See example in Figure 9).

In her presentation to the Research Libraries Discussion Group of the ALA RTSD Serials Section, Marjorie Bloss, former editor of the Rochester Regional Libraries Union List of Serials, described her experience with creating a union list in conformity with national standards.[8] Initially current rules were followed, making a separate record for each manifestation and linking these records with references. As more records were added, representing many different microformats and publishers, the situation became unwieldy. Users were frustrated in their attempts to decipher many records representing the same title. Not only was it expensive to create all the separate records, but the large number of duplicate records, references, and holdings statements caused larger storage fees and higher costs for offline products. Eventually the decision was reached to consolidate the entries into a single record for each serial title, with format designated in the local data record.

A SOLUTION

The Association of Research Libraries was awarded a grant by the National Endowment of the Humanities in 1979 for a project entitled "Bibliographic Control of Materials in Microform." ARL contracted Information Systems Consultants Inc. (ISCI), headed by Richard Boss, to carry out the investigation. While not the primary focus of its report, the ISCI report included recommendations for the descriptive cataloging of reproductions. Anticipating a proliferation of new technologies as well as preservation activities, ISCI "pointed out that future bibliographic records would have to accommodate three or even more formats for a single bibliographic [entity]."[9] ISCI recommended the adoption of a single record approach consisting of several tiers. The primary level would "describe only the intellectual content of the work in terms of such data elements as main entry, title, added entries, subject headings or descriptors, and the year of the intellectual creation of the text." The second tier would include "all aspects of physical description, including imprint and collation of each manifestation of the text."[10] The third and final tier would contain local holdings data.

A variation of this approach has been tested by the Library of Congress. In developing guidelines for the United States Newspaper Project (described in this issue), the Library of Congress concluded that separate records for all printed and microform manifestations of the nation's newspapers would prove expensive and unintelligible. The decision was reached to create a single bibliographic record.

The United States Newspaper project is using the master record

FIGURE 8

Library A (8308,0,5,ʉ, For microfilm see #1234567.) 1-10
   1951-1960

Library B (8301,0,5,ʉ, For hardcopy see #2345678,) 12-20
   1962-1970

Library C (8302,0,4,ʉ, For microfiche see #8765432.) 11-
   1961-

Library D (8212,0,4,ʉ, For microfilm see #1234557. For
   microfiche see #8765432.) 31- 1981-

Library E (3212,3,4,ϵ, Current issues retained until
   microfilm is received. For microfilm see #1234567.)

   or

Library E (8212,0,4,5, Current issues retained until
   microfilm received. For microfilm see #1234567.)

FIGURE 9

```
Library A (8303,0,4,ψ, [Microfilm=1-4 1977-1980
   0,5,ψ]) 5- 1981-

Library B (8303,0,5,ψ, [Microfilm=1-2 1977-1978 0,5,ψ,
   Microfiche=1- 1977- 0,4,ψ]) 3-6 1979-1982

Library C (8303,0,5,ψ [Microfiche=4- 1980- 0,4,ψ])
   1-3 1977-1979

Library D (8303,3,4,6, Current issues retained until
   microfilm is received. [Microfilm=1- 1977- 0,4,ψ])

   or

Library D (8304,0,4,6, Current issues retained until
   microfilm received [Microfilm=1- 1977- 0,4,ψ])
```

convention to account for the various physical forms in which a newspaper may be held. The bibliographic record, in all cases, describes the newspaper as it was originally published. Other physical forms, whether hard copy, film, photoreproduction, etc., are indicated in local data records listing the holdings of participant institutions.[11]

Linda Bartley, CONSER Coordinator at the Library of Congress, reports that this decision has proved very satisfactory.[12]

Cognizant of the expense of duplicate cataloging, disturbed by the inconsistencies in the rules and their applications, and buoyed by the success of the alternative approach in the U.S. Newspaper Project, the Library of Congress has resolved to address the problem further.[13] A contractor has been hired by LC to investigate what is being called "the multiple version problem." The study will include new and/or revised approaches to cataloging and content designation for variant formats of the same work. Significantly, the contractor is specifically directed to investigate the "tiered" model previously recommended in the ISCI study. This model includes (1) primary level bibliographic data; (2) version level bibliographic data; and (3) location/holding level data. The study will address a broad range of "multiple version" issues (including motion pictures with subtitles or dubbing; reprints and facsimile reproductions). LC may then conclude that the "single record" approach is appropriate for all multiple version problems, or only for some specific cases.

All of us who are dissatisfied with current practice should lobby to keep the issue of microform reproductions on the national action agenda. Much time, effort and money are being wasted following the current cataloging practices. A viable alternative has been tested in the United States Newspaper Project. The Library of Congress has demonstrated its willingness to tackle the issue through the commissioning of the "multiple version" study. Let us, as concerned librarians, make sure that the issue of microform reproduction cataloging does not get "set aside" while the admittedly complex problems of other "versions" are investigated. The time to change the national standards is now.

REFERENCE NOTES

1. This controversy is described in exceptionally lucid detail in: *Cataloging Titles in Microform Sets: report of a study conducted in 1980 for the Association of Research Libraries by Information Systems Consultants, Inc.* (Washington, D.C.: Association of Research Libraries, 1983), pp. 29-32, 56-61.
2. Louis Charles Willard, "Microforms and AACR2, Chapter 11: Is the Cardinal Principle a Peter Principle?" *Microform Review* Vol. 10, no. 2 (spring 1981), p. 76.
3. "Library of Congress Policy for Cataloging of Microreproductions," *Cataloging Service Bulletin* No. 14 (fall 1981), pp. 56-58
4. Thomas Bourke, speaking on "Cataloging for Print and Microform Serials: One Record or Two?" American Library Association. Resources and Technical Services Division, Serials Section, Research Libraries Discussion Group, January 6, 1985.
5. Phyllis A. Bruns, *MARC Serials Editing Guide, 2nd CONSER Ed.* (Washington, D.C.: Library of Congress, 1978-), p. 41.
6. *Cataloging Service Bulletin* No. 11 (winter 1981), p. 49.
7. OCLC Union Lists Standards Task Force. *Serial Holdings Statements at the Summary Level: User Guide to the American National Standard.* (Dublin, Ohio: OCLC, 1983), pp. 48-51.
8. Marjorie Bloss, speaking on "Cataloging for Print and Microform Serials: One Record or Two?" ALA RTSD Serials Section Research Libraries Discussion Group, January 6, 1985.
9. *Cataloging Titles in Microform Sets*, p. 57.
10. *Ibid.*, pp. 57-58.
11. Robert Harriman, *Newspaper Cataloging Manual. CONSER/USNP Ed.* (Washington, D.C.: Serial Record Division, Library of Congress, 1984), p. 5.
12. Linda Bartley, speaking on "Cataloging for Print and Microform Serials: One Record or Two?" ALA RTSD Serials Section Research Libraries Discussion Group, January 6, 1985.
13. *Ibid.*

Newspapers and Their Readers: The United States Newspaper Program's List of Intended Audience Terms

James P. Danky

ABSTRACT. The publication by OCLC of the *United States Newspaper Program National Union List* in June, 1985 is an important milestone for librarians in general as well as for participants in the Program and OCLC. The United States Newspapers Program (USNP) is a cooperative venture of the National Endowment for the Humanities and the Library of Congress and will eventually involve libraries in all 50 states and territories. The Program seeks to create an online data base with bibliographic records and holdings statements for all newspapers held in U.S. libraries regardless of their place of publication. To begin with U.S. newspapers are the focus. As the largest union list product produced by OCLC, this nearly 6,000-page set is impressive. However, bulk is not the most important characteristic. By providing access to bibliographic records contributed by many libraries around the nation in new ways, OCLC has responded to patron and librarian demands. The chronological, intended audience (subject), language, and place of publication (geographical) indexes represent the most important advances in access to newspapers in decades. As a prototype, this product holds much promise for the profession, especially in terms of subject access, or intended audience here. This article analyzes the Intended-Audience Index in the first edition, looking at the use of approved and improper terms, describing the origins of the list of terms, and projecting the shape of the data base over the life of the United States Newspaper Program. Like CONSER, of which the USNP is a part, this project is an example of cooperation between many institutions including the Library of Congress, OCLC, and libraries in every state and territory. The article describes one instance of this cooperation in practice.

The publication by OCLC of the first edition of *United States Newspaper Program National Union List June, 1985* was an important milestone in several regards. The Union List contains 25,105 bibliographic records with 37,734 local data records (LDR's) attached, or a

---

James P. Danky, Newspapers and Periodicals Librarian, State Historical Society of Wisconsin.

The author wishes to thank Todd Butler, formerly of OCLC, Inc., and now with the Library of Congress, for supplying advice and information. In addition the author acknowledges the valuable critiques provided by Sandy Berman, Hennepin County Library, and Maureen Hady, Watertown (Wisconsin) Public Library. Lastly, the author is grateful to Clifford Bass, State Historical Society of Wisconsin, for his work on the statistics.

© 1986 by The Haworth Press, Inc. All rights reserved.

ratio of 2:3. The union list was published in both print and microfiche versions. The versions are identical except for the inclusion of the "general" entries in the Intended-Audience Index of the microfiche edition, entries that were deleted in the printed edition, Similarly, the Language index in the microfiche and print versions are identical except for the inclusion of "English" in the microfiche version only. "English", like "general", was omitted from the printed products for reasons of economy and because it provided no effective indexing. Volume 7 contains the Intended-audience and language indexes, and includes some 6,975 entries in the former. The discrepancy between the 6,975 entries in the intended-audience list and the 37,734 entries in the entire list is due to suppressing the term "general" when the union list was printed. In addition, 2,162 local data records lacked an "i" sub-field. The "i" sub-field in the call number of the local data record was created by OCLC specifically to allow for access by Intended-Audience in offline products derived from the U.S. Newspapers Program data base. In the rough draft of the union list, the term "general" occupied pages 61 through 738, with an average of 45 entries per page. This great bulk of 30,759 entries on 677 pages provided no effective indexing capability. However, this is only true of the bound version. The microfiche edition contains all 37,734 entries including "general".

Further, the requirement to assign a term to all "i" sub-fields in the LDR in order to make the union list programs function is under review. Two terms were used in a single "i", or earlier "b", subfield of the LDR by many of the participants at the beginning of the project because the intention was that both terms would be used in creating the Intended-Audience Index. However this has not proven to be the case and thus the second term in the single subfield of the LDR does not figure in either the Index or in the analysis of it. When two terms are entered into two, or more, separate "i" subfields in the LDR both are included in the Index. Any additional discrepancies are due to mathematical projections about the term "general" rather than those fewer instances where the "i" sub-field was not completed. Also, those bibliographic records without LDR's—primary cataloging done in a batch by the Library of Congress in 1982—were not selected and will not be included in any union list until LDR's are created at a future date. The correct use of the list of intended-audience terms by participating libraries is good. Of the 253 terms represented in the June 1985 edition, 115 are approved and 138 improper. However, the inproper terms represent only 453 of the 6975 entries.

When the United States Newspapers Program is complete, the data base is projected to number some 300,000 bibliographic records which will contain some 476,750 LDR's. General-interest newspapers will account for 392,886 (82.4%) of these records and the Intended Audience

Index will not include these as it would be meaningless. But how many Black or German or Abolitionist newspapers will there be in the data base when the project ends?

The List of Intended-Audience Terms was initally developed by the United States Newpapers Program staff at the State Historical Society of Wisconsin but soon grew to include terms submitted by other national repository projects and later by state projects. The goal in producing the List was to create a thesaurus for the USNP that would allow users of the data base to access speciality newspapers by their particular characteristic, for example to locate all newspapers produced by and for the Greenback Party.

The terms on the List were derived from a variety of sources familiar to staff at the State Historical Society of Wisconsin from their earlier bibliographic work. For example in producing the subject indexes to *Women's Periodicals and Newspapers from the 18th Century to 1981: a union list of holdings of Madison, Wisconsin Libraries* (Boston, G.K. Hall, 1982) and *Native American Periodicals and Newspapers, 1828-1982: bibliography, publishing record, and holdings* (Westport, Connecticut, Greenwood Press, 1984) the staff contacted Sanford Berman of the Hennepin County Library for advice. Berman was selected because of his expertise in providing direct and intelligble subject access and he identified both appropriate, existing headings in the Hennepin County system as well as aiding in the development of new headings.

Some of the descriptors differ from those found in *Library of Congress Subject Headings*, 9th edition. For example, LCSH employs BLACK and BLACKS to denote African-descended people outside the U.S. and uses AFRO-AMERICAN and AFRO-AMERICANS to represent U.S. Blacks. The Intended-Audience List uses the term Black to denote U.S. Blacks. Other examples of differences include CHICANO, INUIT, and METIS.

Among the six national repositories selected to be the initial participants in the U.S. Newspapers Program, the State Historical Society of Wisconsin was the logical choice to develop the Intended-Audience List for the USNP. This was based on the Society having completed the two major bibliographic works cited above as well as having done smaller projects on blacks, Asian Americans, and Hispanic Americans.

In developing the List several groups of entries were added from standard sources. For example many participants in the USNP were aware of a large number of religious newspapers in their collections and concern was expressed early on for including names of specific groups. Thus we added in the names of U.S. religious bodies as found in the *Yearbook of American and Canadian Churches* (Nashville, Tennessee: Abingdon Press, 1982). Other terms were derived from the Hennepin County Library authority file. As many of the terms related to established political parties or foreign countries the terms do not vary significantly from similar terms in the Library of Congress Subject Headings, 8th edition.

As a national project, the U.S. Newspapers Program participants offered significant additional terms, terms that could not have been generated by any single project. For example, the Kansas State Historical Society staff encountered many Free Silver newspapers held in their collections and added this term and many others from the numerous political movements that swept the Plains in the nineteenth century.

APPENDIX I

List of Intended-Audience Terms,
including enumerations of their
use in the first edition of
*United States Newspaper Program
National Union List* June, 1985

This list of Ethnic/Political/Religious Focus terms is subject to modifications and additions as needed. Terms denoting nationality may be qualified to indicate whether the group members are American citizens or foreigners living in the U.S. In the first instance, e.g., Armenian Americans; in the second instance, Armenians in America. More than one term can be used if appropriate, e.g., Hispanic, Roman Catholic. However, each term needs to be entered separately in its own "i" subfield.

Additions and corrections may be made to the list by contacting James P. Danky at (608)262-9584 or by writing:

> The State Historical Society of Wisconsin
> 816 State Street
> Madison, WI 53706-1482

PROPER ENTRY USAGES

Instances in Union List

ABOLITIONIST	55
ADVENT CHRISTIAN	
ADVENTIST	
AFGHAN	
AFRICAN see also specific nationalities, e.g., NIGERIAN	
AFRICAN METHODIST EPISCOPAL	
AFRO-AMERICAN see BLACK	
AGRICULTURE	69
ALBANIAN	

ALGERIAN
ALTERNATIVE see UNDERGROUND PRESS 2
AMANA
AMERICAN CARPATHO-RUSSIAN ORTHODOX GREEK
AMERICAN EVANGELICAL CHRISTIAN
AMERICAN INDIAN see NATIVE AMERICAN
AMERICAN LUTHERAN CHURCH
AMERICAN PARTY 8
AMERICAN RESCUE WORKERS
AMISH
ANARCHIST
ANGLICAN see also PROTESTANT EPISCOPAL
ANGLICAN ORTHODOX
ANTI-CATHOLIC see also ANTI-RELIGIOUS 6
ANTI-CLERICAL see ANTI-RELIGIOUS 4
ANTI-MASONIC 30
ANTI-PROHIBITION 2
ANTI-RELIGIOUS
ANTI-SLAVERY 6
APOSTOLIC CHRISTIAN CHURCHES OF AMERICA
APOSTOLIC LUTHERAN CHURCH OF AMERICA
APOSTOLIC OVERCOMING HOLY CHURCH OF GOD
ARABIC   Use for newspapers addressed to the Arab
   community at large. See also names of specific Arabic
   nationalities for those addressed to specific groups 4
ARGENTINIAN see also HISPANIC
ARMENIAN 13
ARMENIAN APOSTOLIC CHURCH OF AMERICA
ARMENIAN CHURCH OF AMERICA
ASSEMBLIES OF GOD
ASSOCIATE REFORMED PRESBYTERIAN
ASSYRIAN 1
AUSTRALIAN
AUSTRIAN 1

BAHAI FAITH
BALTIC see ESTONIAN; LATVIAN; LITHUANIAN
BAPTIST GENERAL CONFERENCE 3
BAPTIST'S FREE WILL see FREE WILL BAPTISTS
BAPTIST MISSIONARY ASSOCIATION OF AMERICA 3
BASQUE 1
BELGIAN (non-Flemish)   Use only for non-Flemish Belgian
   groups. For Belgian-Flemish groups see FLEMISH.
BELORUSSIAN Use for publications specifically addressed to

the Belorussian ethnic community. See RUSSIAN for those addressed to the Russian community as a whole.
BETHEL MINISTERIAL ASSOCIATION
BIBLE CHURCH OF CHRIST
BIBLE PROTESTANT CHURCH
BIBLE WAY CHURCH OF OUR LORD JESUS CHRIST WORLD WIDE, INC.
BLACK 596
BOHEMIAN see also CZECHOSLOVAK 47
BOLIVIAN see also HISPANIC
BRAZILIAN see also HISPANIC 1
BRETHREN IN CHRIST CHURCH
BRITISH see also ENGLISH, WELSH, CORNISH, MANX, SCOTTISH 5
BUDDHIST
BULGARIAN 1
BULGARIAN EASTERN ORTHODOX
BURMESE
BUSINESS see also INDUSTRY 13
BYELORUSSIAN see BELORUSSIAN

CAMBODIAN see KAMPUCHEAN
CANADIAN see also FRENCH-CANADIAN; METIS 1
CANADIAN REBELLION, 1838 see MACKENZIE'S REBELLION
CARPATHO-RUTHENIAN see also UKRANIAN 1
CATHOLIC see ROMAN CATHOLIC 7
CHICANO see also HISPANIC 5
CHILEAN see also HISPANIC
CHINESE see also TAIWANESE 32
CHRISTADELPHIANS
CHRISTIAN AND MISSIONARY ALLIANCE
CHRISTIAN CHURCH (DISCIPLES OF CHRIST)
CHRISTIAN CHURCHES AND CHURCHES OF CHRIST
CHRISTIAN METHODIST EPISCOPAL
CHRISTIAN SCIENTIST 6
CHURCH OF GOD OF PROPHESY
CHURCH OF CHRIST, SCIENTIST see CHRISTIAN SCIENTIST
CHURCH OF GOD
CHURCH OF GOD IN CHRIST
CHURCH OF JESUS CHRIST OF THE LATTER DAY SAINTS see MORMON
CHURCH OF THE BRETHREN

CHURCHES OF CHRIST	
CIVILIAN CONSERVATION CORPS	
COLOMBIAN see also HISPANIC	
COMMUNIST	3
CONGREGATIONALIST see UNITED CHURCH OF CHRIST	
CONSERVATIVE BAPTIST ASSOCIATION OF AMERICA	
COPTIC	
CORNISH see also BRITISH	
COSTA RICAN see also HISPANIC	
CROATIAN	21
CUBAN see also HISPANIC	
CUMBERLAND PRESBYTERIAN	
CZECHOSLOVAK	9
DAHOMEY	
DANISH	54
DEMOCRAT	1346
DOMINICAN	
DOUKHOBOR	
DUTCH	9
EAST INDIAN see also HINDU	
ECUADORIAN see also HISPANIC	
EGYPTIAN see also ARABIC	
EL SALVADORAN see also HISPANIC	
ENGLISH see also BRITISH	52
EPISCOPAL	1
ERITREAN	
ESKIMO see INUIT	
ESTONIAN	
ETHIOPIAN see also ERITREAN	
EUGENICS	
EVANGELICAL	
EVANGELICAL CHRISTIAN	1
EVANGELICAL LUTHERAN	
EVANGELICAL METHODIST	
FARMERS' ALLIANCE	29
FEDERALIST	21
FILIPINO	
FINNISH	16
FLEMISH	2
FREE SILVER	9
FREE SOIL PARTY	23
FREE-STATE (Party)	8

FREE WILL BAPTISTS 1
FRENCH 104
FRENCH-CANADIAN see also CANADIAN 3

GEORGIAN
GERMAN 596
GHANAIAN
GRANGE see PATRONS OF HUSBANDRY
GREEK 9
GREEK ORTHODOX
GREENBACK 45
GUATEMALAN see also HISPANIC
GYPSY

HAITIAN
HAWAIIAN 24
HEBREW see JEWISH
HINDU
HISPANIC see also specific nationalities, e.g., GUATEMALAN, 18
  NICARAGUAN, MEXICAN, etc.
HMONG
HONDURAN see also HISPANIC
HUNGARIAN 41
HUTTERITE

ICELANDIC see also SCANDINAVIAN
INDEPENDENT 90
INDIAN, AMERICAN see NATIVE AMERICAN
INDIAN, EAST see EAST INDIAN
INDIAN, WEST see WEST INDIAN
INDONESIAN
INDUSTRY see also BUSINESS
INUIT
IRANIAN
IRAQI
IRISH 45
ISLAMIC see MUSLIM
ISRAELI
ITALIAN 103

JAMAICAN see also WEST INDIAN
JAPANESE 24
JEHOVAH'S WITNESS
JEWISH see also ISRAELI 51
JORDANIAN see also ARABIC

KAMPUCHEAN	
KNOW NOTHINGS see AMERICAN PARTY	
KOREAN	1
KU KLUX KLAN	12
LABOR	162
LAOTIAN	
LATINO see HISPANIC	
LATTER-DAY-SAINT see MORMON	
LATVIAN	3
LEBANESE see also ARABIC	
LIBERIAN	
LIBYAN	
LITHUANIAN	20
LOYALIST	8
LUTHERAN use only if no more specific denomination is given	3
LUTHERAN CHURCH IN AMERICA	
LUTHERAN CHURCH, MISSOURI SYNOD	
LUXEMBOURG	1
MACEDONIAN	
MACKENZIE'S REBELLION	3
MALTESE	
MANX see also BRITISH	
MARITIME	
MARXIST see COMMUNIST; SOCIALIST	
MENNONITE	2
METHODIST	7
METIS	
MEXICAN see also HISPANIC	26
MEXICAN AMERICAN see CHICANO	
MILITARY	33
MOLOKANE	
MORAVIAN see also CZECHOSLOVAK	
MORMON	15
MOROCCAN see also ARABIC	
MOSLEM see MUSLIM	
MUGWUMP	2
MULTI-ETHNIC To be used when a newspaper applies to all ethnic groups. Do not use if addressed to two or more specific groups, e.g., to the Puerto Ricans and Cubans.	
MUSLIM	1
NATIONAL BAPTIST CONVENTION	
NATIONAL REPUBLICAN	25

NATIVE AMERICAN see also INUIT   31
NEGRO see BLACK
NICARAGUAN see also HISPANIC
NIGERIAN
NORWEGIAN see also SCANDINAVIAN   98

ORTHODOX PRESBYTERIAN

PAKISTANI
PALESTINIAN see also ARABIC
PANAMANIAN see also HISPANIC
PARAGUAYAN see also HISPANIC
PATRIOT'S WAR see MACKENZIE'S REBELLION
PATRONS OF HUSBANDRY
PENTECOSTAL
PEOPLE'S PARTY   1
PERUVIAN see also HISPANIC
PHILIPINO see FILIPINO
PILLAR OF FIRE
PLYMOUTH BRETHREN
POLISH   61
POLITICAL REFORM see REFORM MOVEMENTS
POPULIST   123
PORTUGUESE   5
PRESBYTERIAN   27
PRIMITIVE BAPTIST
PRIMITIVE METHODIST
PROGRESSIVE   4
PROGRESSIVE PARTY   2
PROHIBITIONIST   94
PRO-SLAVERY   3
PROTESTANT   6
PROTESTANT EPISCOPAL see EPISCOPAL
PUERTO RICAN see also HISPANIC
PURITAN

QUAKER see RELIGIOUS SOCIETY OF FRIENDS

REFORM MOVEMENTS
REFORMED CHURCH
RELIGIOUS SOCIETY OF FRIENDS
REPUBLICAN   1338
ROMAN CATHOLIC   30
ROMANIAN   7
ROMANIAN ORTHODOX EPISCOPATE
ROMANY see GYPSY

ROSICRUCIAN	
RUSSIAN	27
RUSSIAN ORTHODOX	
SALVADORAN see EL SALVADORAN	
SCANDINAVIAN see also specific nationalities, e.g. SWEDISH	25
SCOTTISH see also BRITISH	1
SECOND ADVENTIST	
SERBIAN	16
SEVENTH-DAY ADVENTIST	
SEXUAL REFORM see REFORM MOVEMENTS	
SHAKER	
SILESIAN	
SIAMESE see THAI	
SLAVERY see PRO-SLAVERY, ABOLITIONIST	
SLOVAKIAN	23
SLOVENIAN	34
SOCIALIST use only if no more specific designation is made; see also ANARCHIST; COMMUNIST	40
SOCIALIST LABOR PARTY	1
SOCIALIST PARTY	3
SOCIALIST WORKERS PARTY	
SOUTHERN BAPTIST CONVENTION	
SOUTHERN METHODIST	
SPANISH use only for people of Spanish descent	63
STATES RIGHTS	
SUDANESE	
SWEDENBORGIAN	
SWEDISH see also SCANDINAVIAN	59
SWISS	2
SYRIAN	
TAIWANESE	
TEMPERANCE see PROHIBITIONIST	6
THAI	
TORY	
TRANSYLVANIAN SAXONS	10
TRINITARIAN	
TUNISIAN see also ARABIC	
TURKISH	
UGANDAN	
UKRAINIAN	12
UKRAINIAN CATHOLIC	1
UNDERGROUND PRESS	

UKRAINIAN ORTHODOX
UNION see LABOR
UNION LABOR PARTY 2
UNITARIAN
UNITED CHURCH OF CHRIST 1
UNITED METHODIST CHURCH
UNITED PENTECOSTAL CHURCH INTERNATIONAL
UNITED PRESBYTERIAN
URUGUAYAN see also HISPANIC

VENEZUELAN see also HISPANIC
VETERANS 3
VIETNAMESE
VOLUNTEERS OF AMERICA

WELSH see also BRITISH 3
WESLEYAN
WEST INDIAN see also JAMAICAN
WHIG 347
WISCONSIN EVANGELICAL LUTHERAN SYNOD
WOMEN 3
WOMEN'S SUFFRAGE 1

YIDDISH see JEWISH 4
YUGOSLAVIAN see CROATIAN, SERBIAN, SLOVENE

IMPROPER ENTRY USAGES

Abolishionist	1
Abolistionist	1
Abolition	1
Agricultural	3
American	5
Anti-Abolitionists	1
Anti-Black	4
Anti-Catholic, Socialist	1
Anti-Jeffersonian	1
Anti-Monopolist	2
Anti-Monopoly	3
Anti-Monopoly party	2
Anti-Prohibitionist	1
Anti-Tammany	2
Arab American	1
Baptist	15
Black American	1

Black Suffrage	1
Campaign Paper	1
Canadian Independence	1
Cherokee	2
Chinese-American	2
Christian	3
Collegiate	13
Commercial	7
Commercial and Financial	1
Convict	1
Czech	13
Danish American	3
Deaf-Mutes	1
Democrat 1836–1856	1
Democratic	38
Democratic Party	1
Democratic Republican	15
Episcopal Methodist	1
Evening ed.	1
Federal Republican	1
Feminist	1
Frech-American	1
Free Soil	4
French-American	9
Gays	1
German American	47
German American Bund	4
German, Roman Catholic	1
German, Socialist	2
Grand Army of the Republic	3
Greek-American	2
Greenback, Anti-Monopolist	1
Greenback, Democrat	2
Greenback, Labor	1
Hispanic American	1
Hungarian American	11
Imperialist	2
Independent Republican	1
Independent-Republican 1879–1885	1
Industrial	4
Irish American	1
Irish in America	2
Irish, Catholic	1
Italian American	2

Japanese American	20
Jeffersonian Republic	1
Jeffersonian Republican	1
Jewish American	1
Jewish, German	2
Know Nothing	5
Legal	2
Legislative Proceedings	1
Lesbians	1
Liberal	2
Liberty Party	2
Literary	11
Literature	2
Literature, Lottery	1
Livestock Raising	2
Maritime	1
Mechanics	2
Methodist-Episcopal	1
Mexican-American	6
Monopolies	1
Nationalist	2
Nativist	3
Newspaper 84/18th Century cage	1
Newspaper 84/932	1
Norwegian American	29
Norwegian-Danish	3
Ordnance works	2
People's Party, Labor	2
Phonetics	1
Portugese	1
Potuguese	1
Pro-Republican	1
Progressive Republican	1
Prohibition	8
Prohibitionists, reformers	1
Protectionist	1
Railroad ed.	1
Railroads	1
Rechabite	2
Reform movements	1
Reoublican	1
Republica	1
Republican, 1857–1901	1
Republican, 1886–1898	1

Republican, 1896–1918	1
Roman Cathlic	1
Ruthenian	1
Saturday ed.	3
Second evening edition	1
Semiweekly ed.	1
Share the Wealth Society	5
Skandinavaian	1
Slovak	9
Slovene	1
Socialism	1
Socialist labor	2
Socialist, anti-war	1
Spiritualism	1
Spiritualists	1
Sport news	1
Sports	1
Strike paper	3
Suffrage	1
Sunday ed.	2
Swedish-American	9
Swiss American	1
Triweekly ed.	1
Tuesday ed.	2
Underground	1
Union	1
Union Labor	1
Universalist	3
Wed. ed.	1
Whig Democrat	1
Whig, Legislative proceedings	2
Women, labor	1
Y.M.C.A.	

PROPER ENTRY USAGES

Abolitionist	55
Agriculture	69
Alternative	2
American Party	8
Anti-Catholic	6
Anti-Clerical	4
Anti-Masonic	30

Anti-Prohibition	2
Anti-Slavery	6
Arabic	4
Armenian	13
Assyrian	1
Austrian	1
Baptist General Conference	3
Baptist Missionary Association of America	3
Basque	1
Black	596
Bohemian	47
Brazilian	1
British	5
Bulgarian	1
Business	13
Canadian	1
Carpatho-Ruthenian	1
Catholic	7
Chicano	5
Chinese	32
Christian Scientist	6
Communist	3
Croatian	21
Cuban American	1
Czechoslovak	9
Danish	54
Democrat	1346
Dutch	9
English	52
Episcopal	1
Evangelical Christian	1
Farmer's Alliance	29
Federalist	21
Finnish	16
Flemish	2
Free Silver	9
Free Soil Party	23
Free Will Baptists	1
Free-State (Party)	8
French	104
French-Canadian	3
German	596
Greek	9
Greenback	45

Hawaiian	24
Hispanic	18
Hungarian	41
Independent	90
Irish	45
Italian	103
Japanese	24
Jewish	51
Korean	1
Ku Klux Klan	12
Labor	162
Latvian	3
Lithuanian	20
Loyalist	8
Lutheran	3
Luxembourg	1
Mackenzie's Rebellion	3
Mennonite	2
Methodist	7
Mexican	26
Military	33
Mormon	15
Mugwump	2
Muslim	1
National Republican	25
Native American	31
Norwegian	98
People's Party	1
Polish	61
Populist	123
Portuguese	5
Presbyterian	27
Pro-Slavery	3
Progressive	4
Progressive Party	2
Prohibitionist	94
Protestant	6
Republican	1338
Roman Catholic	30
Romanian	7
Russian	27
Scandinavian	25
Scottish	1
Serbian	16

Slovakian	23
Slovenian	34
Socialist	40
Socialist Labor Party	1
Socialist Party	3
Spanish	63
Swedish	59
Swiss	2
Temperance	6
Transylvanian Saxons	10
Ukranian	12
Ukranian Catholic	1
Union Labor Party	2
United Church of Christ	1
Veterans	3
Welsh	3
Whig	347
Women	3
Women's suffrage	1
Yiddish	4

Following is a breakdown of the top 50 entries out of the 6975 non-general Intended Audience entry usages:

TOP 50 ENTRIES	P.E.U.	I.E.U.	% P.E.U.	% I.E.U.	% E.U.
Democrat	1346	-	20.638		19.297
Republican	1338		20.515		19.183
Black	596		9.138		8.545
German	596		9.138		8.545
Whig	347		5.320		4.975
Labor	162		2.484		2.323
Populist	123		1.886		1.763
French	104		1.595		1.491
Italian	103		1.579		1.477
Norwegian	98		1.503		1.405
Prohibitionist	94		1.441		1.348
Independent	90		1.380		1.290
Agriculture	69		1.058		0.989
Spanish	63		0.966		0.903
Polish	61		0.935		0.875
Swedish	59		0.905		0.846
Abolitionist	55		0.843		0.789
Danish	54		0.828		0.774
English	52		0.797		0.746
Jewish	51		0.782		0.731
Bohemian	47		0.721		0.674
German American		47		10.375	0.674

Greenback	45	0.690		0.645
Irish	45	0.690		0.645
Hungarian	41	0.629		0.588
Socialist	40	0.613		0.573
Democratic		38	8.389	0.545
Slovenian	34	0.521		0.487
Military	33	0.506		0.473
Chinese	32	0.491		0.459
Native American	31	0.475		0.444
Anti-Masonic	30	0.460		0.430
Roman Catholic	30	0.460		0.430
Farmer's Alliance	29	0.445		0.416
Norwegian American		29	6.402	0.416
Presbyterian	27	0.414		0.387
Russian	27	0.414		0.387
Mexican	26	0.399		0.373
National Republican	25	0.383		0.358
Scandinavian	25	0.383		0.358
Hawaiian	24	0.368		0.344
Japanese	24	0.368		0.344
Free Soil Party	23	0.353		0.330
Slovakian	23	0.353		0.330
Croatian	21	0.322		0.301
Federalist	21	0.322		0.301
Japanese American		20	4.415	0.287
Lithuanian	20	0.307		0.287
Hispanic	18	0.276		0.258
Finnish	16	0.245		0.229

Note: Plural forms have been collapsed into singular form.

TOTAL PROPER ENTRIES:	115
TOTAL IMPROPER ENTRIES:	138
GRAND TOTAL ENTRIES:	253
TOTAL PROPER ENTRY USAGES:	6522
TOTAL IMPROPER ENTRY USAGES:	453
GRAND TOTAL ENTRY USAGES:	6975

Following is a breakdown of the top 50 entries out of the projected 83,350 non-general Intended Audience entry usages:

TOP 50 ENTRIES	P.E.U.	I.E.U.	% P.E.U.	% I.E.U.	% E.U.
Democrat	16084		20.638		19.297
Republican	15989		20.515		19.183
Black	7122		9.138		8.545
German	7122		9.138		8.545
Whig	4147		5.320		4.975
Labor	1936		2.484		2.323
Populist	1470		1.886		1.763

French	1243		1.595	1.491
Italian	1231		1.579	1.477
Norwegian	1171		1.503	1.405
Prohibitionist	1123		1.441	1.348
Independent	1075		1.380	1.290
Agriculture	825		1.058	0.989
Spanish	753		0.966	0.903
Polish	729		0.935	0.875
Swedish	705		0.905	0.846
Abolitionist	657		0.843	0.789
Danish	645		0.828	0.774
English	621		0.797	0.746
Jewish	609		0.782	0.731
Bohemian	562		0.721	0.674
German American		562	10.375	0.674
Greenback	538		0.690	0.645
Irish	538		0.690	0.645
Hungarian	490		0.629	0.588
Socialist	478		0.613	0.573
Democratic		454	8.389	0.545
Slovenian	406		0.521	0.487
Military	394		0.506	0.473
Chinese	382		0.491	0.459
Native American	370		0.475	0.444
Anti-Masonic	358		0.460	0.430
Roman Catholic	358		0.460	0.430
Farmer's Alliance	347		0.445	0.416
Norwegian American		347	6.402	0.416
Presbyterian	323		0.414	0.387
Russian	323		0.414	0.387
Mexican	311		0.399	0.373
National Republican	299		0.383	0.358
Scandinavian	299		0.383	0.358
Hawaiian	287		0.368	0.344
Japanese	287		0.368	0.344
Free Soil Party	275		0.353	0.330
Slovakian	275		0.353	0.330
Croatian	251		0.322	0.301
Federalist	251		0.322	0.301
Japanese American		239	4.415	0.287
Lithuanian	239		0.307	0.287
Hispanic	215		0.276	0.258
Finnish	191		0.245	0.229

Note: Plural forms have been collapsed into singular form.

TOTAL PROPER ENTRIES:	115
TOTAL IMPROPER ENTRIES:	138
GRAND TOTAL ENTRIES:	253
PROJECTED TOTAL IMPROPER ENTRY USAGES:	77,937

PROJECTED TOTAL IMPROPER ENTRY USAGES:	5,413
PROJECTED GRAND TOTAL ENTRY USAGES:	83,350

APPENDIX II

BIBLIOGRAPHY ON THE UNITED STATES NEWSPAPER PROGRAM

Note: This bibliography is selective and does not include newspaper articles about state projects or articles on the pre-1982 aspects of the United States Newspapers Program as cataloging was not an active concern.

Butler, Todd. "U.S. Newspaper Program Gains Momentum," *OCLC Newsletter*, no. 158 (July, 1985) p. 6–7
_____. "U.S. Newspaper Program National Union List Available," *OCLC Newsletter*. no. 159 (Oct., 1985) p.8
_____. "United States Newspaper Program Workshops," *CONSER: Conversion of Serials*. no. 10 (June, 1985), p. 2–3
_____. "November U.S. Newspaper Program Meeting Highlights," *CONSER: Conversion of Serials*. no. 8 (April, 1984) p. 32–4
Cannon, Harold. "The National Endowment for the Humanities and the United States Newspapers Program," *Cataloging & Classification Quarterly*. vol. 6, no. 4 (summer, 1986) p.
Cole, James E. "AACR2 and the Newspaper Cataloging Manual: a comparison," *Cataloging & Classification Quarterly*. vol. 6, no. 4 (Summer, 1986) p.
Danky, James P. "Newspapers and Their Readers: The United States Newspaper Program's List of Intended Audience Terms," *Cataloging & Classification Quarterly*. vol. 6, no. 4 (Summer, 1986) p.
Everett, Diana and Bobby Weaver. "The Texas Newspaper Project," *Texas Libraries*. vol. 44, no. 3 (July, 1983) p. 98–102
Graham, Crystal. "Rethinking National Policy for Cataloging Microforms Reproductions," *Cataloging & Classification Quarterly*. vol. 6, no. 4 (Summer, 1986) p.
Hady, Maureen E. "Cataloging Oklahoma Newspapers at the State Historical Society of Wisconsin for the U.S. Newspaper Projects," *Oklahoma Librariar*. vol. 33, no. 5 (Sept./Oct., 1983) p. 47–48
Harriman, Robert B. "Coordination of Cataloging Practices in the United States Newspapers Program," *Cataloging & Classification Quarterly*. vol. 6, no. 4 (Summer, 1986) p.
_____. *Newspaper Cataloging Manual; CONSER/USNP Edition*. Washington, Library of Congress, 1984. 95p. Update No. 1 (1985), 1p.
The Indiana Newspaper Messenger: a report of the Indiana Newspaper Project. Bloomington, Indiana. no. 1 (Dec. 1984)-. Insert to *Focus on Indiana Libraries*.
Leibowitz, Faye and Cathy Sorensen. "Perspectives on the Pennsylvania Newspapers Project at the University of Pittsburgh," *Cataloging & Classification Quarterly*. vol. 6, no. 4 (Summer, 1986) p.
Newspapers in California. Sacramento, California: California State Library Foundation, 1985. 176p.
Newspapers in New York: recommendations for an initial statewide plan of data collecting and entry prepared for the New York State Library. Stoughton, Wisconsin: James Danky & Associates, 1983. 25p.
Newspapers of New York State: a statewide plan for bibliographic control and preservation, final report of the Task Force on Newspaper Bibliography and Preservation. Albany, New York: New York State Library, 1981. vi, 38, 13p.
O'Donnell, Francis J. "Yesterday's Newspapers," *Humanities*. vol. 4, no. 3 (August, 1983) p. 4–5

The Pennsylvania Newspaper Project Reporter. Harrisburg, Pennsylvania. Number 1 (August, 1983)-.

Ruth, Marcia. "Our *Razzoopers* are Worth Saving!," *Presslines.* vol. 6, no. 9 (Sept., 1984) p. 13

Schieber, Phil. "U.S. Newspapers Program—An Extra for Scholars," *Research Libraries in OCLC: A Quarterly.* no. 11 (July, 1983) p. 5–12.

Utah's Newspapers, Traces of Her Past: papers presented at the Utah Newspaper Project Conference, University of Utah, November 18, 1983. Edited by Robert P. Holley; with checklist of Utah newspapers compiled by Dennis McCargar, edited by Yvonne Stroup. Salt Lake City, Utah: Marriott Library, University of Utah, 1984. 319p.

Wilson, Rebecca A. and Lydia Suzanne Kellerman. "Challenges of On-Site Cataloging," *Cataloging & Classification Quarterly.* vol. 6, no. 4 (Summer, 1986) p.

Wisdom, Donald F. "Newspaper Program Developments," *Library of Congress Information Bulletin.* vol. 42, no. 21 (May 23, 1983) p. 167.

CATALOGING NEWS

Walter M. High, News Editor

The "Cataloging News" section of *Cataloging & Classification Quarterly* is designed to be an information exchange column for catalogers. The consistently strong attendance at the various cataloging discussion group meetings of ALA indicates a desire for information sharing, but few of us are able to attend national conferences on a regular basis. There is a need to bring this type of sharing into print so that all may benefit from it. The purpose of this column is to gather cataloging information and news that may not otherwise reach the national audience it deserves.

To be successful, this column depends upon a national network of people willing to funnel cataloging news to us. We will accept unsolicited material for inclusion in the column provided it fits within the defined scope. You are encouraged to submit items as follows:

1. *Notes*: minutes and/or summaries of cataloging conferences, workshops, meetings, symposia, lectures, and other gatherings that present information of interest to catalogers. If only a portion of such a meeting is devoted to cataloging, submit notes on that portion only.
2. *Announcements*: flyers or descriptions of new cataloging aids, courses, and workshops on cataloging, and special cataloging projects recently undertaken.
3. *Grants*: detailed descriptions of grants that relate to cataloging (including those for retrospective conversion of cataloged materials).
4. *Brief communications*: descriptions of policies and/or procedures that may be of interest to other catalog librarians, organizational patterns that affect cataloging workflow, and comments on the art or state of cataloging as currently practiced.

Please include written permission to reproduce your material in whole or in part for the column. Address all correspondence to: Walter High,

News Editor, *CCQ*, Box 7111, D. H. Hill Library, North Carolina State University, Raleigh, NC 27695-7111.

This month's column is devoted exclusively to the individual cataloging phase projects of the United States Newspaper Program. The Program has received surprisingly little publicity since it began in 1980, and the important statewide projects have gotten almost no acclaim. This column is an attempt to rectify that omission.

The projects of the cataloging phase are the real meat of the Program. One envisions catalogers all over the country sitting before microfilm readers and dusting the cobwebs off old volumes of newspapers as they painstakingly compile the bibliographic information needed to create full MARC records for these titles. The reports from project directors are full of exciting discoveries of previously unknown titles and enthusiasm for the goals of the Program. One senses the pride these people take in bringing scholarly resources to the attention of the academic community.

Cataloging & Classification Quarterly is pleased to be able to shine the spotlight on this diverse group of catalogers scattered about the country as they struggle to achieve bibliographic control over newspapers. The following summaries came from the project directors in response to a questionnaire from *CCQ*.

THE LIBRARY OF CONGRESS

The Library of Congress acquires, catalogs, and preserves approximately 33,000 newspapers published in Western European languages. About 12,000 of these are United States newspapers covering the period from 1704 to the present. As a result of the Interagency Agreement between the Library of Congress and the National Endowment for the Humanities, the Library of Congress (1) lends advice on proposal development, (2) ensures adherence to cataloging and preservation standards, (3) provides training, coordination, and technical support for cataloging and preservation activities,(4) chairs the United States Newspaper Program Technical Committee, and (5) coordinates computerized data entry of bibliographic and holdings information into the CONSER network.

Project Director: Frank J. Carroll, Head, Newspaper Section
Personnel: Robert Harriman
Todd Butler
Funding: No special funding
Completion date: December 31, 1986
Titles involved: 12,000 (est.)

Contributions: The Library of Congress makes three contributions to the United States Newspaper Program that are unique. The Library was the first large research library to provide full bibliographic records of its newspaper holdings, and also the first to catalog these titles as MARC records. The project at the Library of Congress developed a comprehensive cataloging manual solely for newspapers (which has been used extensively by other USNP grantees). The Library, in cooperation with OCLC, adopted the master bibliographic record convention that accounts for the various physical formats in which a newspaper may be held. By the time the National Endowment for the Humanities funded the first project grant in 1982, the Library of Congress had already cataloged 2,200 titles.

AMERICAN ANTIQUARIAN SOCIETY

The goal of the American Antiquarian Society is to produce machine-readable records for its pre-1877 American newspaper titles and to add holdings for these titles to the CONSER database through OCLC according to the *Newspaper Cataloging Manual*, ACCR2, and the *CONSER Editing Guide* (2nd ed.). These records will contribute to a national database of bibliographic and holdings information for American newspapers. Libraries, researchers, and other projects will have access to this data through the national bibliographic utilities and through publications such as the recently published *United States Newspaper Program Union List*.

Project Director:	Joyce Ann Tracy, Curator of Newspapers and Serials
Personnel:	Joseph Macmanus, Senior Cataloger
	Martha Gunnarson, Cataloger
	Anne Moore, Cataloger
	Susan Wolfe, Cataloger
Funding:	$162,458 (National Endowment for the Humanities)
	$223,898 (renewal of grant)
Completion date:	January 31, 1987
Titles involved:	13,500–14,000

Contributions: The American Antiquarian Society's collection of newspapers is one of the finest in the world and its pre-1821 holdings are preeminent. The pre-1877 collection contains more titles than that of the Library of Congress. Because of this fine resource, the Society helped bring the attention of the National Endowment for the Humanities to the value of newspaper collections in national repositories. The Endowment decided that repositories with varied holdings from distinct geographic areas would be useful for pilot projects in the early stages of the United States Newspaper Program. As a result, the American Antiquarian Society and five other original grantees studied and modified the newspaper cataloging rules, collaborated with LC and OCLC to create and enter machine-readable newspaper records into the database, and developed holdings statements. These actions helped establish ground rules and standards for the bibliographic phase of the United States Newspaper Program. Although the majority of the Society's holdings are pre-1877, it collects newspapers from Western states through 1895. These later titles and holdings will not be entered into the OCLC CONSER database as part of this project.

KENTUCKY NEWSPAPER PROJECT

The bibliographic control phase of the Kentucky Newspaper Project (KNP) will inventory, catalog, and collect information for the preservation of United States newspapers permanently retained in Kentucky. KNP personnel are now cataloging the newspapers at the University of Kentucky at Lexington, site of the largest collection in the state (approximately 1,400 titles). They will then visit each of the estimated 300 other newspaper repositories in the state.

Project Director: Judy A. Sackett
Personnel: Margaret E. Potts, Assistant Project Director and Cataloger
Mary H. Welch, Senior Cataloger
Dr. Charles Czarski, Field Cataloger
Funding: $142,136 (National Endowment for the Humanities)
$119,822 (University of Kentucky)
Completion date: August 31, 1987
Titles involved: 3,325 (est.)

Contributions: Despite the presence of extensive newspaper collections throughout Kentucky, access to holdings information has been difficult. No statewide union list has been compiled since the mid-1930's, and that list included only twenty-two institutions. Newspaper microfilming began at the University of Kentucky Library in 1954. The UK Microfilm Center continues to film all but twenty of the approximately 180 newspapers currently published in the state; the microfilm for the remainder is purchased from commerical vendors. The information collected through the Kentucky Newspaper Project will make possible the most complete and accurate guide ever produced for Kentucky. The bibliographic information, coupled with preservation efforts planned for the third phase of the project, will provide the most complete control for Kentucky newspaper holdings ever collected.

PENNSYLVANIA NEWSPAPER PROJECT

The Pennsylvania Newspaper Project will locate and catalog about 10,000 Pennsylvania newspaper titles that are held in approximately 1,400 repositories, including academic, public, special, and school libraries; historical societies; publishers; and private collections. The bibliographic and holdings data will be entered into the OCLC database. Activities are decentralized, but under the general direction of the State Library. The University of Pittsburgh performs CONSER reviewing. Cataloging sites will be maintained during the first two years at the State Library, the Historical Society of Pennsylvania (Philadelphia), the Pennsylvania State University, the University of Pittsburgh, and repositories to be selected in northwestern and northeastern Pennsylvania. Each site is responsible for inventorying collections held in an assigned group of counties. As each county is completed, a "want list" of titles published but not found is prepared and published. When working in a library that does not have access to OCLC, staff will use portable microcomputers to dial-access OCLC and to search state-developed lists of titles already cataloged.

Project Director: David R. Hoffman, Library Services Director, State Library of Pennsylvania

Personnel: Susan Bryson, Newspaper Cataloger, State Library of Pennsylvania

Faye Leibowitz, Newspaper Cataloger, University of Pittsburgh

Suzanne Thomas, Serials Cataloger, University of Pittsburgh

Cathy Sorenson, Newspaper Cataloger, University of Pittsburgh

Sue Kellerman, Newspaper Cataloger, Pennsylvania State University

Rebecca Wilson, Newspaper Cataloger, Pennsylvania State University

Barbara Kurimchak, Newspaper Cataloger, Historical Society of Pennsylvania

Funding: $312,418 (National Endowment for the Humanities)
                      $81,275 (Cost Sharing)
Completion date: December, 1988
Titles involved: 10,000 (est.)

Contributions: Pennsylvania's newspapers provide a unique record of its history. They begin with the *American Weekly Mercury* of 1719, and include many that document the movement toward independence from Great Britain. A wide range of foreign-language papers cover the movement of immigrants through the port of Philadelphia to all parts of Pennsylvania and to the West and South. Other newspapers, some of national stature, some of tiny communities, reflect labor, ethnic, and cultural heritages.

WEST VIRGINIA NEWSPAPER PROJECT

The purpose of the West Virginia Newspaper Project is to locate, preserve, and establish bibliographic control over all newspapers published in West Virginia and the part of Virginia that became West Virginia in 1863. Bibliographic data for these newspapers will be entered into the CONSER database through OCLC to create an online union catalog.

Project Director: Harold M. Forbes, Curator
Personnel: Susan Beates Hansen
                      Jeanne S. Grimm
Funding: $88,051 (National Endowment for the Humanities)
                      $41,648 (West Virginia University)
Completion date: September 30, 1986
Titles involved: Over 1,020 from West Virginia
                      Over 250 from other states

Contributions: The Project will provide the first statewide union list of West Virginia newspapers, and preserve many unique newspaper files. When the project is completed, a comprehensive guide to West Virginia newspapers will be published. Every significant file of West Virginia newspapers will be preserved on microfilm.

INDIANA NEWSPAPER PROJECT

The goals of the Indiana Newspaper Project are to locate or create bibliographic records for every newspaper held at public repositories in

Indiana, and to create comprehensive holdings records for each title cataloged.

Project Director:	Sally Rausch, Associate Dean for Technical Services, Indiana University Libraries
Personnel:	Gary Charbonneau, Project Manager, Serials Department, Indiana University Libraries
	Lois Upham, Original Cataloger, Indiana State Library
Funding:	$228,773 (National Endowment for the Humanities)
	$138,773 (cost sharing, contributions)
Completion date:	March, 1988
Titles involved:	2,900 (est.)

Contributions: Although the number of Indiana newspapers has declined in recent years, newspaper publishing in the state retains a vitality that is unusual elsewhere: only four states have more dailies that still publish. Newspapers reflect the history and heritage of Indiana and the entire country, and the Indiana Newspaper Project will make a major contribution to the preservation of that heritage.

HAWAII NEWSPAPER PROJECT

The aim of the Hawaii Newspaper Project is to research, catalog, and record holdings for Hawaii's newspapers, which date back to 1834. Hawaii's press reflects the multi-ethnic nature of its population, and includes newspapers in eight languages. The holdings of the following repositories are represented: University of Hawaii, Bishop Museum, Archives of Hawaii, Hawaiian Historical Society, Hawaii Mission Children's Society, and the Hawaii State Library System.

Project Director:	John Haak, University Librarian, University of Hawaii
Personnel:	Nancy Morris, Manager
	Sophia McMillen, Cataloger
	Larry Osborne, Editor
Funding:	$49,900 (including University of Hawaii cost-sharing)
Completion date:	December, 1985
Titles involved:	375

Contributions: Undoubtedly, the unique contribution of the Hawaii project to the national newspaper database is the addition of some 75

Hawaiian language newspapers, which document Hawaiian thought and culture over the past 150 years. A more significant body of literature in this far-from-dead language can scarcely be imagined. Equally interesting in content, however, are the newspapers produced by other ethnic groups in Hawaii, which record issues and events in the Polynesian kingdom as it moved toward American statehood.

Among the Project's exciting discoveries is that of a previously unknown second volume of Hawaii's very first newspaper, the Hawaiian-language *Ka Lama Hawaii*. It was found in the Bishop Museum, when the frayed binding of a totally unrelated title revealed the rare Hawaiian treasure. Also, the Project is on the trail of files of several pre-World War II Japanese newspapers that no longer exist in Hawaii. Many of these were destroyed in the frightening days of Pearl Harbor, but seem to have survived in Japan and California.

ALABAMA NEWSPAPER PROJECT

The goals of the Alabama Newspaper Project are to identify titles, locate and inventory holdings, and achieve bibliographic control over a maximum number of Alabama newspapers; to raise general awareness of the usefulness of Alabama newspapers as an historical resource and increase their availability to the public; to publish a guide to Alabama newspapers that will serve as an historical reference for students, researchers, and other users; and to prepare for the preservation of Alabama newspapers on microfilm in the successive phases of the project.

The planning phase of the Project took place from July 1 to December 31, 1983. Its accomplishments included a questionnaire survey of some 650 repositories; an initial listing of 3,600 newspapers published in Alabama since 1812; and a compilation of a bibliography of some 300 sources relating to Alabama newspapers. Both of these have been updated and published in a combined interim reference guide.

The bibliographic phase commenced on October 1, 1984. Five major repositories, Auburn University, the Alabama Department of Archives and History, Birmingham Public Library, Samford University, and the University of Alabama, are cataloging their holdings for entry into OCLC's database. Project authentication of OCLC newspaper records for CONSER is performed centrally by the project cataloger. Original cataloging by repositories is assigned by oldest and most complete holdings in case of duplicate title holdings. Holdings at sites other than the five major repositories are surveyed for on-site data collection. This is performed by volunteer data collectors under the supervision of the project coordinator. Approximately 900 Alabama titles have been entered into OCLC, and some 430 new records have been authenticated for CONSER.

Project Director:	Dr. Edwin C. Bridges, Alabama Department of Archives and History
Personnel:	Paul E. Martin, Coordinator, Auburn University
	Rickie Brunner, Cataloger, Alabama Department of Archives and History
Funding:	$150,000 (National Endowment for the Humanities)
Completion date:	September 30, 1987
Titles involved:	3,100 (est.)

Contributions: The Project will perform bibliographic entry for hundreds of uncataloged Alabama newspapers, and will provide bibliographic records for many newspapers published by blacks that have been relatively unknown to the research community. Also, it will concentrate the energies of hundreds of individuals and institutions on a common goal of preserving the state's newspaper heritage. These services will generate awareness of a great historical resource, little used in the past, that will soon be available to all.

CENTER FOR RESEARCH LIBRARIES NEWSPAPER PROJECT

The Center for Research Libraries Newspaper Project's goals were (1) to improve bibliographic access to CRL's U.S. newspapers; (2) to enter into the CONSER database records for the more than 1,000 U.S. newspaper titles held by CRL; (3) to enter detailed holdings records for these titles into the USNP union list on OCLC, NEPU (holdings records were also entered into two other union lists on OCLC: the Center's own, CRIU, and the Serials of Illinois Libraries Online, SILO); (4) to upgrade existing records in OCLC, when found, through the use of CONSER authorization; (5) and to produce machine-readable records for these titles, which may be used to create specialized lists, COM catalogs, etc.

Project Director:	Donald B. Simpson
Personnel:	Karla D. Petersen, Manager
	Judith A. Sandstrom, Supervisor
	Adriana Pilecky, Cataloger
Funding:	$35,095 (National Endowment for the Humanities)
	$8,930 (Center for Research Libraries)
Completion date:	July, 1983

papers, and a number of special interest group titles. The Project provided access to the extensive and unique collection of ethnic newspapers held by CRL, many of which are represented by complete or nearly complete files, or are the most extensive or only files known to exist.

MONTANA HISTORICAL SOCIETY

The Montana Historical Society aims to survey state and selected national repositories for their holdings of Montana newspapers, to catalog and enter into OCLC the bibliographic and holdings information for all Montana newspapers located, to produce a microfiche union catalog of these newspapers, and to microfilm significant papers discovered in locations other than the Society as well as important, unfilmed runs in the Society's collection.

Project Director: Robert M. Clark
Personnel: Kathryn Otto, Cataloger
David Spencer, Clerical Assistant
Funding: $84,569 (National Endowment for the Humanities)
$18,000 (Federal matching funds)
Completion date: April 30, 1986
Titles involved: 900 (est.)

Contributions: Because it had the first state project to be funded under the U.S. Newspaper Program, Montana has helped develop some of the national guidelines, especially on technical cataloging matters. The project may well make Montana the state with the most complete newspaper record available—almost all of it on microfilm. It has discovered twenty-eight titles not previously represented in the Society's collection, mostly very small or even single-issue runs, and missing issues for forty-five other titles. All newly discovered issues are being microfilmed. The Project has added roughly 225 reels to available Montana newspaper resources. By August, 1985, cataloging and inputting of 618 titles was completed and 1,008 local data records showing holdings had been created.

RUTGERS UNIVERSITY

The goal of the Rutgers University project is to complete the cataloging of all United States newspapers held on its five campuses. This cataloging will be entered into the OCLC database and provide many of the records needed by other institutions for a statewide project in New Jersey.

Project Director: Ilona S. Caparros
Personnel: Lida Sak, Senior Cataloger
Jodie A. Brown, Project Cataloger
Funding: $140,000
Completion date: June 30, 1986 (may be delayed several months)
Titles involved: 3,000 (est.)

Contributions: A major strength of the Rutgers newspaper collection is its extensive holdings of New Jersey titles, including an impressive sampling of papers that represent important eras in American history, such as the Civil War. The Alexander Library on the New Brunswick campus houses rare items in its Special Collections Department. These newspapers will become available to researchers nationwide once the Project is completed.

KANSAS NEWSPAPER PROJECT

The Kansas Newspaper Project is being conducted as a national repository project in which only the holdings of the Kansas State Historical Society are cataloged. Besides contributing to the national effort, the project fulfills the Society's need for bibliographic control. (The last comprehensive bibliography of the collection was published in 1916.) The newspaper collection has grown by leaps and bounds since then. A card catalog to provide subject access is being created by the Historical Society Library in conjunction with this project.

Project Director: Eugene D. Decker, State Archivist
Personnel: Rebecca Schulte, Manager
Cheryl Riley, Cataloger
Jane Forkner, Cataloger
Dorothy Hancock, Cataloger
Funding: $232,038
Completion date: December 31, 1986
Titles involved: 11,154 (est.)

Contributions: The Project has made several that are unique. It developed an inventory data sheet as well as a plan of action, and created inventory forms for 14,863 serial titles. Non-newspapers were included as well as newspapers, since the task of deciding which publications truly are newspapers ultimately rests with the catalogers. Moreover, the addition of the Kansas newspapers themselves should be considered a unique contribution to the national union list. The world should know about such titles as the *Cain City Razooper*, *The Rose of Sharon* from Sharon Springs, Kansas, *The Bazoo*, *Thomas County Cat*, *The Unmuzzled Truth*, and the *Astonisher & Paralyzer*.

UTAH NEWSPAPER PROJECT

The Utah Newspaper Project provides improved bibliographic control over Utah newspapers by surveying holdings within the state and in selected national repositories, by furnishing cataloging information to the OCLC database, by creating a union list of all newspapers held in Utah, and by disseminating the resulting information.

Project Director: Robert P. Holley
Personnel: Yvonne Stroup, Librarian
Mitch Mounteer, Library Assistant Support Staff
Funding: $109,102 (National Endowment for the Humanities)
$31,820 (cost sharing)
Completion date: September 30, 1986
Titles involved: 1,900–2,000

Contributions: The planning phase of the Utah Newspaper Project had as one of its principal results a checklist of Utah newspapers cited in secondary sources. Building upon this list of 920 titles, the University of Utah will catalog its own holdings of 344 newspapers while seeking further title and holdings information from other libraries, archives, newspaper offices, and historical museums in Utah, as well as selected national repositories. The Project will enter bibliographic data into the OCLC database through a limited CONSER membership, and will provide full MARC-S records according to CONSER standards. Furthermore, it will create a union list of all newspapers held in Utah through the OCLC union list capability. While it will give first priority to Utah's published newspapers, the Project will also enter into the union list and catalog, where needed, an estimated 500 out-of-state newspapers. Preliminary research indicates that Utah libraries have significant holdings of Idaho and Nevada newspapers.

STATE HISTORICAL SOCIETY OF WISCONSIN

The State Historical Society of Wisconsin was one of the six national repositories selected for the initial phase of the United States Newspaper Program. The Society has the second largest collection of newspapers in the United States, after the Library of Congress, and includes titles from the seventeenth century to the present, and from every state and territory. The collection also contains significant holdings from all Canadian provinces and territories.

Project Director: James P. Danky
Personnel: Charles McMorris, Senior Newspaper Cataloger
Maureen Hady, Cataloger
Jeanne Fondrie, Cataloger
Ann Cashin, Cataloger
Funding: $350,000 (National Endowment for the Humanities)
Completion date: January, 1987
Titles involved: 5,820 (through October, 1985)

Contributions: This extensive collection of newspapers is becoming available for researchers as the Society adds its holdings to the OCLC database. The Society was the first CONSER participant in Wisconsin and has long been known for the quality of its cataloging. The first edition of OCLC's *United States Newspaper Program National Union List* contains these records and provides access by language, title, place of publication, date, and intended audience. Such a wide number of access points should substantially increase the use of these newspapers by researchers.

Additional newspaper cataloging projects are in progress or have been completed with funding from the National Endowment for the Humanities or a Title II-C grant of the Higher Education Act. The following institutions did not furnish information on their projects:

The Iowa State Historical Society
The New York State Historical Society
The New York State Library
The Western Reserve Historical Society
The Virgin Islands Bureau of Libraries
The Boston Public Library